As the deer pants for streams of water,

so my soul pants for you, O God.

My soul thirsts for God, for the living God.

When can I go and meet with God?

(Psalm 42:1-2 NIV)

OTHER BOOKS BY JAMES W. SIRE

The Universe Next Door

Scripture Twisting

How to Read Slowly

The Discipleship of the Mind

Jesus the Reason

Chris Chrisman Goes to College

Why Should Anyone Believe Anything at All?

Habits of the Mind

Václav Havel

Naming the Elephant: Worldview as a Concept

Why Good Arguments Often Fail

A Little Primer on Humble Apologetics

James W. Sire

Learning to Pray
Through the Psalms

IVP Books

An imprint of InterVarsity Press
Downers Grove, Illinois

InterVarsity Press
P.O. Box 1400, Downers Grove, IL 60515-1426
World Wide Web: www.ivpress.com
E-mail: email@ivpress.com

InterVarsity Press® *is the book-publishing division of InterVarsity Christian Fellowship/USA*®, *a movement of students and faculty active on campus at hundreds of universities, colleges and schools of nursing in the United States of America, and a member movement of the International Fellowship of Evangelical Students. For information about local and regional activities, write Public Relations Dept., InterVarsity Christian Fellowship/USA, 6400 Schroeder Rd., P.O. Box 7895, Madison, WI 53707-7895, or visit the IVCF website at <www.intervarsity.org>.*

Design: Cindy Kiple
Images: iStockphoto

ISBN 978-0-8308-3332-0

Printed in the United States of America ∞

 InterVarsity Press is committed to protecting the environment and to the responsible use of natural resources. As a member of the Green Press Initiative we use recycled paper whenever possible. To learn more about the Green Press Initiative, visit <www.greenpressinitiative.org>.

Library of Congress Cataloging-in-Publication Data

Sire, James W.
    Learning to pray through the Psalms: a guide for individuals and
groups/James W. Sire
        p. cm.
    Includes bibliographical references and index.
        ISBN 0-8308-3332-3 (pbk.: alk. paper)
    1. Bible. O.T. Pslams—Devotional use. 2. Bible. O.T. Psalms
—Prayers. 3. Prayer—Christianity. I. Title.
BS1430.54.S57 2005
223'.2'0071—dc22   *2005018632*

| P | 20 | 19 | 18 | 17 | 16 | 15 | 14 | 13 | 12 | 11 | 10 | 9 | 8 | 7 | 6 | 5 |
| Y | 23 | 22 | 21 | 20 | 19 | 18 | 17 | 16 | 15 | 14 | 13 | 12 | 11 | 10 | 09 |

To Eugene Peterson and Dallas Willard

spiritual mentors through their books

Contents

Acknowledgments.   9

Introduction 11

  I   BECOMING RIGHT WITH GOD—*Psalm 32* 17

  2 WAITING FOR THE LORD—*Psalm 130*. 36

  3 NIGHT THOUGHTS—*Psalm 4*. 54

  4 A MORNING MEDITATION—*Psalm 5* 68

  5 THIRSTING FOR GOD—*Psalms 42—43*. 84

  6 A PLEA FOR DELIVERANCE FROM SLANDER—*Psalm 7* . . 112

  7 A BLAZING SONG OF JOY—*Psalm 84*. 128

  8 PRAYING OUR ANGER—*Psalm 137*. 146

  9 THE GOD WHO KNOWS ME—*Psalm 139*. 177

10 OUR MIGHTY FORTRESS—*Psalm 46*. 196

11 TEACH US TO PRAY 209

Appendix: *Guide for Small Group Leaders*. 216

Notes. 219

Annotated Bibliography. 224

Acknowledgments

How can I not begin without thanking our great God who inspired the psalmists and gave us those marvelous records of the prayers of the ancient Hebrews! This book is a meditation and an encouragement to meditation prompted by the texts of those who poured out their souls to God. So thanks quickly go to those hearty souls who wrote the psalms and displayed for us such a vast panorama of human thought and emotion, thus freeing us so many centuries later to bare our heart and mind before the God who fashioned us and intended us to be like himself.

From a more recent perspective, I also want to thank a host of biblical and theological scholars who by their publications have helped me grasp the original meaning of the psalms and suggested their modern relevance. Chief among them is Eugene Peterson, whose notion of the psalms as *answering speech* suggested the basic approach of this book. Following quickly is Dallas Willard, whose work on spirituality sets this book's theological backdrop. Thanks also go to longtime friend and seminary professor Larry Sibley, who read the manuscript at an early stage. As acquiring editor, Cindy Bunch was a delight to work with. Ruth Goring, as she always does, improved the manuscript at the final stage. Finally, thanks to those many who must remain nameless because, while what I have learned from them is embedded in this book, the source has long been forgotten.

Introduction

I remember it clearly. One afternoon in 1952 I was standing on the corner of Tenth and P in Lincoln, Nebraska, waiting for a bus. Okay, maybe it was another corner nearby, and maybe I was waiting for something else. But it was Lincoln and I was waiting.

I had a brand-new copy of a brand-new translation of the Old Testament in two volumes. In my hand was the volume with the Psalms. I haphazardly opened to Psalm 108 and read, "My heart is ready, O God. My heart is ready." The words leaped off the page, capturing with utter immediacy the state of my soul. I don't know if I had recognized this state before I read those words, but when I read them, I knew. My heart was ready. My heart was ready for God. And I was learning to pray through the psalms.*

I imagine that something like this has happened to myriads of men and women over the centuries. A psalm is read privately or heard publicly in a worship service, and the hearer/listener says deep in his or her heart, "Yes, yes, oh yes. This is what I want to say to God." From their origin in ancient Israel thousands of years ago, the psalms have indeed been the *answering speech* of God's people.

It is my primary goal in the present book to make more explicit this *answering* character of the biblical psalms and to prompt learning how we

---

*Source materials are listed in the notes section, arranged by page number and key words.

might more profoundly employ these psalms as our own speech—speech that reflects not just a generic reaction but our own utterly intimate response. May the psalms become our own individual answering speech!

There are three aspects to this goal: (1) to learn what the psalms say about and do with prayer, (2) to learn to pray by means of the psalmists' words and (3) to develop a way of praying psalms with others.

READING COMES FIRST

Our response to God through the psalms first demands that we read them and that we read them well. So each chapter begins with a different psalm. Each of these psalms is, as Eugene Peterson says, an answering speech— the psalmist's response to God coming out of his own and his community's situation. It is, in other words, a particular response to a particular set of circumstances. Nonetheless, one of the glories of the psalms is that while they have a very particular origin in time and space—ancient Israel—they are universal in application. The presentations here focus on this mysterious connection: the way the ancient becomes modern and we twenty-first-century worshipers come to participate in the common worship of a God who never changes and yet is new to us every morning.

As mysterious as this process is, it does have a certain logic. That is, there are ways to proceed: we can learn and practice, or better, learn and practice and then learn from our practice. The present book is more like instructions for riding a bike than a presentation of a theory of prayer. It is my sincere desire that you will learn not so much from reading this book as from practicing its suggestions. That is why "Teach Us to Pray" looks as if it should be an introduction but is, in fact, the book's conclusion. Everything in that chapter should already have become obvious. Readers who have "practiced" the book should themselves be able to write the final chapter.

What then is the logic of this mysterious process? It all begins with reading. The sequence is this:

1. reading, rereading, then reading again—and again

2. clarifying the text, gaining an understanding of each of the words or phrases that seem puzzling

3. analyzing the structures in the psalm: (a) rational structure, i.e., the flow of ideas; (b) emotional structure, i.e., the flow of emotions evoked in and by the psalm; (c) rhetorical structure

4. achieving a sense of the psalmist's own often complex and changing relationship to God (e.g., calm, joyous, disturbed, turbulent, angry, depressed)

5. making the answering speech of the psalmist one's own, by repeating his words as one's own, adapting his words to one's own situation or doing some of both

The first stage, reading, is the most important. Only when we have grasped the psalm so deeply that we think its thoughts and feel its emotions are we ready to make it our own answering speech. The process puts strong emphasis on the initial, almost prerational act of reading the text, because this is the only way we can avoid second-guessing the meaning of the psalm. If we skip to analysis before absorbing the psalm, we are likely to be writing our own psalm—not just "our" psalm but one that is counter to that of the psalmist. Good readers yield to the text well before they become its analysts and critics.

Disciplined reading and rereading is a simple act of intensive looking—a looking to see what is actually there. Louis Agassiz, a Harvard zoologist of a hundred years ago, was famous for the way he introduced new students to laboratory work. He would begin by "handing them a dead fish, or some other specimen, and requiring them to produce a complete and accurate description of it before he allowed them to proceed. To meet Agassiz's standards, this sometimes took weeks, and left the students with a badly decomposed fish on their hands." Of course, it is unlikely that any of us will come to know as much about any psalm we read as the students came to know about their fish. But that is not the goal. The goal is for each of us to know the psalm as well as we can. In the end we will not be left with a decomposed psalm; rather the psalm will have worked its way with us, attaining a clarity of meaning that brings us joy.

Stages two and three, clarifying and analyzing, lead to stage four and then quite naturally to stage five. Little has changed in human nature since the psalms were written. We readily see ourselves in the psalmists. In most cases their answering speech readily becomes our own.

There is, however, one set of psalms that often cause difficulty for followers of Christ. These are the so-called imprecatory psalms, in which the psalmist calls down God's vengeance on his enemies. I have chosen to face this difficulty head on in chapter eight, dealing with Psalm 137. Even where we find the psalmist's words horrifying, I think as we pray through them with care we will find that they ring true. This psalm will test our willingness to grapple with our own anger.

SPIRITUAL DISCIPLINE

Prayer is, of course, a spiritual discipline, however it is practiced. That is, it is a means God uses to grow and intensify our relationship with him. Moreover, prayer is closely related to other spiritual disciplines, especially the disciplines of silence and solitude. Each chapter in this book assumes that each reader is alone or at least undistracted by other people. You will be encouraged to be silent or to wait—that is, to stop the running inner dialogue we have with ourselves throughout any normal day.

To be silent means to refrain from talking, to refrain from paying attention to the sounds around us, to turn off the TV, the radio, the CD player, and to seek a quiet place for paying attention solely to God and to what he may send into our mind. This is not a normal habit for most of us in the Western world. We are a wordy people, and we seek the sounds of the marketplace and not the sounds of silence. But only as we make ourselves available to God through reading his Word and waiting for him to cast our attention his way will we mature in the practice of the spiritual disciplines and in the character of our spiritual life.

The difference between talking about silence and practicing it is like the difference between learning about prayer and praying. Only the practice contributes to spiritual growth. In the chapters that follow you will be directed to spend much time in silence with psalms that I trust God will use to transform your character and bring you closer to him.

I will say no more about this. I only encourage you to start the process as the next chapter directs.

PRAYING THE PSALMS IN COMMUNITY

Most of this book concentrates on private reading and praying. But the psalms can also be prayed in community. In ancient Israel many of the psalms were used in community worship. They are still used in the liturgies and prayer books of many Christian denominations.

Each chapter includes a group leader's guide and liturgy for that psalm. The appendix is a general guide for leaders of small groups.

But let's face it. The instructions in this book will not bring you a richer experience of God's presence. Spiritual fruit will come only if you actually pray through the psalms. And so to Psalm 32 . . .

Becoming Right with God
Psalm 32

Do you remember the first time you realized you'd done something wrong? Maybe it was when you were reaching your hand into the proverbial cookie jar and suddenly it crashed to the floor. Now you had to face Mom. How did your agony get resolved? Or did it?

Recall now that you stand before the holy God. You know you've not always pleased him with your behavior. How do you feel? In Psalm 32 we come to see our situation in bold relief and understand its impact on our soul. Still, if we let this psalm sink into our soul, not only will our relationship to God be restored, but we will be learning to pray with a community of saints that stretches back to ancient Israel. And we will be learning how to pray through any psalm.

Psalm 32 has long been a part of my spiritual furniture. So let me introduce you to it in a way I hope will lead you into a constantly growing understanding, not just of this psalm but of almost every psalm you learn to pray.

The best way to approach any reading is simply to begin. In most cases, whether we are reading a sacred or a secular text, we don't need an introduction by an expert. After all, we have already chosen a particular psalm, poem, novel or essay. We have our reason for choosing it. So we just read.

INITIAL READING OF PSALM 32

Psalm 32

Of David. A Maskil.

¹Happy are those whose transgression is forgiven,
　　whose sin is covered.
²Happy are those to whom the LORD imputes no iniquity,
　　and in whose spirit there is no deceit.

³While I kept silence, my body wasted away
　　through my groaning all day long.
⁴For day and night your hand was heavy upon me;
　　my strength dried up as by the heat of summer.

Selah

⁵Then I acknowledged my sin to you,
　　and I did not hide my iniquity;
I said, "I will confess my transgressions to the LORD,"
　　and you forgave the guilt of my sin.

Selah

⁶Therefore let all who are faithful
　　offer prayer to you;
at a time of distress, the rush of mighty waters
　　shall not reach them.
⁷You are a hiding place for me;
　　you preserve me from trouble;
　　you surround me with glad cries of deliverance.

Selah

⁸I will instruct you and teach you the way you should go;

I will counsel you with my eye upon you.
[9]Do not be like a horse or a mule, without understanding,
    whose temper must be curbed with bit and bridle,
    else it will not stay near you.

[10]Many are the torments of the wicked,
    but steadfast love surrounds those who trust in the LORD.
[11]Be glad in the LORD and rejoice, O righteous,
    and shout for joy, all you upright in heart.

This first reading is just the beginning. Read the psalm again, this time more slowly. Then read it for a third time. Read it until the words seep easily into your conscious mind. With each reading, observe and absorb the words and sentences, the images and ideas. Do this with a completely open mind, without prejudging what it is the psalmist is concerned for.

You will find yourself resonating with some parts of the psalm more than others. Certain words or pictures will pop into your mind. Some will be pleasant, some painful, some enticing you to settle into the reading with more attention, some causing you to hold back, even to resist what seem to be the implications for your own life. But neither draw conclusions nor harbor reservations. Let the words, sentences and ideas work on you.

It is important not to analyze the text too soon, not to reach a settled judgment about what it is saying, especially what it is saying to you. There will be plenty of time for that later. In these initial readings, let down your defenses and let the psalm work on you. Let it paint its holy picture on your soul. You are listening to the voice of God through the voice of the psalmist. You can trust this voice. So you mustn't presume to judge even what that voice is saying, especially what it is saying to you. You must first *hear* the voice, and that requires attention, an intentional leaning of the soul toward

God. At the beginning, this sort of reading is a discipline—a spiritual discipline—requiring effort. With repeated practice over weeks and months, this way of reading and hearing will become second nature.

GETTING AT THE MEANING OF PSALM 32

Such initial readings are the foundation for any really fruitful understanding of a psalm—or for that matter any poetry or highly intense form of writing. They help prevent our reading into the text (what the scholars call *eisegesis*) rather than reading out from it *(exegesis)*. Only the latter will assure our grasping what God is saying to us through the words of the ancient writers.

Still, we should not think we have read well if we do not go deeper. We need to move on from a basic absorption of the text to a fuller understanding by the mind and a richer experience in the emotions. Several steps are involved. They do not need to be taken in any particular order; in fact, in the final analysis they merge as the mind and emotions grasp the results of these steps in one single act of apprehension. We then can recognize, and talk about, the impact of Psalm 32 on our spiritual life as a unitary experience. In other words, to get at the meaning of the psalm, we take it apart, then put it back together. Or, better, God leads us to see the parts so clearly that we see the whole more fully.

So what are the parts we need to examine? They include the *rational structure*, the *emotional structure*, the *meanings* of the individual words and the implicit *context* of the psalm. Let's take up each of these in turn.

The Meaning of the Words

This is an easy psalm to understand. We scarcely need the comments of scholars, important as they are for understanding many biblical texts. Except for two words we will look at shortly, there are no odd words or names of obscure places or people. The key words give name to basic ideas: our problems with *transgression, sin, iniquity, deceit, guilt,* and the solutions of *confession, forgiveness, deliverance.*

But there are some arresting personal images—our body *wasting away,* God's *heavy hand* on us, our strength being *dried up by the heat of summer.* There's also a vivid image of nature in turmoil—*the rush of mighty waters.* To modern readers, this picture of our human plight is almost comic, but we are likely to find it apt nonetheless. We are *horses* and *mules* who have to be *bridled* lest we charge off to our own destruction.

Only two words invite a comment from scholars. The first is *Selah.* That's a transliteration from Hebrew, not a translation. Though it appears seventy-one times in Psalms and three times in Habakkuk, no one has figured out exactly what it means. As the *New Bible Dictionary* says, scholars generally hold that it is a musical or liturgical sign "whose precise import is not known." Its presence gives evidence that this particular psalm was set to music or was part of a liturgy. Since there is no way to judge its significance, we can ignore its presence in the poem.

The second word is the first one in the poem: *happy.* Translators have not quite resolved whether the Hebrew word should be translated *happy* or *blessed. Blessed* seems too formal, too religious, too distant from our experience. On the other hand, *happy* seems too common, signaling an emotion that is too ordinary. When God reaches down with his marvelous forgiving grace, his absolutely unmerited favor toward us, we are surely more than merely *happy.* We are something else too. We have been endowed with something touching the divine. We have been *blessed.* Another way to see the difference is to see the contrasts to both. *Happy* contrasts with *sad,* while *blessed* contrasts with *cursed.* Surely it is better to be *blessed* than to only be *happy.* It is this more profound state of being that is being signaled. So let's stick with *blessed.*

Overall Rational Structure

The rational structure of a psalm or poem is the structure or flow of its main ideas. In the case of Psalm 32, this structure is easy to discern. There is a new set of ideas in each set of verses.

The happy state of those who are forgiven

¹Happy are those whose transgression is forgiven,
> whose sin is covered.

²Happy are those to whom the LORD imputes no iniquity,
> and in whose spirit there is no deceit.

The painful state of those who are unforgiven

³While I kept silence, my body wasted away
> through my groaning all day long.

⁴For day and night your hand was heavy upon me;
> my strength dried up as by the heat of summer.

> > *Selah*

Confession and its results

⁵Then I acknowledged my sin to you,
> and I did not hide my iniquity;
> I said, "I will confess my transgressions to the LORD,"
> and you forgave the guilt of my sin.

> > *Selah*

God's protection of his people

⁶Therefore let all who are faithful
> offer prayer to you;
> at a time of distress, the rush of mighty waters
> shall not reach them.

⁷You are a hiding place for me;

you preserve me from trouble;
you surround me with glad cries of deliverance.

Selah

God's word to his people
[8]I will instruct you and teach you the way you should go;
I will counsel you with my eye upon you.
[9]Do not be like a horse or a mule, without understanding,
whose temper must be curbed with bit and bridle,
else it will not stay near you.

Concluding moral and sustaining counsel
[10]Many are the torments of the wicked,
but steadfast love surrounds those who trust in the LORD.
[11]Be glad in the LORD and rejoice, O righteous,
and shout for joy, all you upright in heart.

Psalm 32 has a clear progression of ideas. It begins with the declaration of how things are in God's world—the happiness of the forgiven and unhappiness of the unforgiven—and proceeds to the solution for the unforgiven and on through an affirmation of the protection of God, his counsel to all people and a concluding moral.

Emotional Structure
Psalm 32 also has an emotional structure. It begins in happiness and ends in joy, but in between there is profound agony. Notice the progress:

- happiness (vv. 1-2)
- agony (vv. 3-4)
- a yielding spirit (v. 5)
- a turn to thankful, expectant prayer (v. 6)

- a slowly returning sense of the peace of God's deliverance (v. 7)
- a reflective acceptance of God's counsel (vv. 8-9)
- a survey of the course of emotions (v. 10)
- a joyful ending shout (vv. 10-11)

The emotions themselves, however, do not drive the psalm. They follow the lead of the ideas. Because of the consequences of sin, we groan; because of the consequences of forgiveness, we find comfort, peace and joy.

Through this psalm we are learning about prayer—both the conditions that should prompt prayer and the prayer that should be prompted. Sin leads to torment; confession leads to deliverance. The equation is simple, and the implication for us is clear. We know that we are among the sinners; we therefore need to confess.

THE IMPLICIT CONTEXT OF THE PSALM

The psalm is a straightforward poem, a Hebrew hymn, used perhaps in some worship ceremonies. The presence of *Selah* marking the ends of some verses suggests such communal use. But unlike Psalm 51, which is prefaced by a historical note relating it to King David and his affair with Bathsheba, Psalm 32 does not contain any obvious allusions to specific sinners or their sins. It is in this sense a generic psalm, readily adaptable to current use by both individuals and communities. After all, we all sin and we all need to confess. The whole pattern of the psalm is universally human.

PRAYING PSALM 32

Most knowledge worth knowing involves doing. This is as true in the spiritual life as it is in swimming, painting or writing a novel. One cannot become a nuclear physicist by merely reading physics texts. One must read the books, to be sure, but then one must become attached to a mentor, enter a laboratory and begin slowly to act like a physicist.

Yes, we may have slowly absorbed Psalm 32, understood its words and observed its rational and emotional structure. But when we pray in its light, we come to know by doing. We put ourselves in the way of God's doing for us what he has done for the psalmist and countless others over the past several millennia.

What follows here, then, is a guide to such a prayer.

Read through the entire psalm again. Then with eyes open, read and pray section by section.

> [1]Happy are those whose transgression is forgiven,
> > whose sin is covered.
> [2]Happy are those to whom the LORD imputes no iniquity,
> > and in whose spirit there is no deceit.

Respond: *O Lord, I know in my mind that this is true. Write this truth on my heart. Burn it on my soul.* Add your own reflections on these two verses.

> [3]While I kept silence, my body wasted away
> > through my groaning all day long.
> [4]For day and night your hand was heavy upon me;
> > my strength dried up as by the heat of summer.
> > > > > > *Selah*

Respond: *Lord, I hear the psalmist proclaim the agony of his soul. I would not have thought to put it in these words, but I know his situation well. I too have felt the effect of my guilt.* In your own words, describe to God how you have felt under his watchful eye.

> [5]Then I acknowledged my sin to you,
> > and I did not hide my iniquity;
> I said, "I will confess my transgressions to the LORD" . . .

Respond: *I have (often) made confession of my sins. But I do so now again, not just the ones I know but the faults that I have hidden and blocked from consciousness. You know my sins—all of them—and I do not want to try any longer to hide them from myself. The knowledge of them may crush me, and I may groan as I recall them, but I want to put before you a slate of sins that you can forgive and erase without trace. Bring them now to mind.* Begin to place before God, first, all those sins you easily remember and, second, those he brings to mind now.

Pause in inner silence for five to ten minutes. Let what you have confessed settle down. Let your emotions (whatever they now are) relax. Then continue to read:

. . . And you forgave the guilt of my sin.

Respond: *Yes, as Jesus said on the cross, it is finished—done, over. You have forgiven me.* Pause in silence for a time. Do you feel the peace of God flow through you? Are you amazed that God forgives? Then respond: *Thank you! Thank you! Thank you!* . . . Rest for some moments in his acceptance. Then read:

> ⁶Therefore let all who are faithful
>   offer prayer to you;
>   at a time of distress, the rush of mighty waters
>   shall not reach them.
> ⁷You are a hiding place for me;
>   you preserve me from trouble;
>   you surround me with glad cries of deliverance.
>
> Selah

Respond: *These words, Lord, are my words too. They are not just my words; they are and will be a message I will give to my Christian friends. You have preserved me, delivered me. You have also delivered them. I will encourage my community of faith,* (name of your community here), *to pray in times of distress, especially the distress caused by sin.*

You are my hiding place. You shield me from the trouble of temptation. When I remember your presence and focus on your care for me, I can stand firm in your way.

I am curious about the glad cries of deliverance that surround the psalmist. Where do they come from? Are they the voices of your angels? I can almost hear them, rejoicing for a sinner's repenting. So I too rejoice, and I thank you! Thank you! Thank you!

Then read:

> [8]I will instruct you and teach you the way you should go;
> I will counsel you with my eye upon you.
> [9]Do not be like a horse or a mule, without understanding,
> whose temper must be curbed with bit and bridle,
> else it will not stay near you.

Who speaks these lines? Is it the psalmist? Or is it you, Lord? I think it's your voice the psalmist is transmitting here. I know your eye is upon me. Not only do you know what I do right and wrong, but you know me, for your eye is on me. I can trust you.

Your counsel is certainly sound. I am indeed much too much like an unruly horse, chafing at the bit, straining against the bridle, resisting the reins. May I yield to your direction!

Keep inner silence now. Reflect on those things God is putting on your mind, things that you should do or stop doing, attitudes you should cultivate or lay aside. In your inner soul, yield to his direction. Then read:

> [10]Many are the torments of the wicked,
> but steadfast love surrounds those who trust in the LORD.
> [11]Be glad in the LORD and rejoice, O righteous,
> and shout for joy, all you upright in heart.

Respond: *Thank you, Lord, for pointing out your place in my life as my Creator, my Redeemer, the lover of my soul, the lover of all of me.* Shout it out: *Praise God! Hallelujah!*

SOME FURTHER REFLECTIONS

Praying Psalm 32, no matter how intently we have done so, does not end our need for confession. We may expect to find ourselves gradually—sometimes suddenly—getting rid of some of our sinful tendencies and behavior. We can look forward to substantial improvement, but not perfection, at least not on this side of glory, until God completely purifies our soul.

An expression I heard years ago sums it up. We are saved, being saved and yet to be saved. That is, we are saved from the penalty of sin (utter separation from God forever); we are being saved from the power of sin (usually gradually); we are yet to be saved from the presence of sin. In the middle time of being saved from the power of sin, we will find ourselves yielding to temptation and will feel frustrated because of that. But if we continue to return to God, pray for his forgiveness and discipline ourselves, we will find a growing satisfaction in our relationship with God, a growing joy of life in his presence and a growing hope of the coming of the kingdom of God—God's entire reign over all things bright and beautiful, all creatures great and small.

> Be glad in the LORD and rejoice, O righteous,
>   and shout for joy, all you upright in heart.

Or as Eugene Peterson paraphrases these lines in *The Message*:

> Celebrate Yahweh!
>   Sing together—everyone!
>   All you honest hearts, raise the roof!

LEARNING TO PRAY THROUGH THE PSALMS IN COMMUNITY

Each of the psalms presented in this book can be prayed in community as well as by individuals. In fact, some if not all of them were written for communal use in various ceremonies in Hebrew communities. Even those that seem to us late Western-minded people to be solely individual may have been intended for the Hebrew people as a whole, the "I" being a stand-in for Israel as a nation.

Eugene Peterson puts great emphasis on prayer as a communal activity:

> The assumption that prayer is what we do when we are alone—the solitary soul before God—is an egregious, and distressingly persistent, error. We imagine a lonely shepherd on the hills composing lyrics to the glory of God. We imagine a beleaguered soul sinking in a swamp of trouble calling for help. But our imaginations betray us. We are a part of something before we are anything, and never more so than when we pray. Prayer begins in community.

This does not mean that we should not pray alone. Jesus himself often went off by himself, away from his disciples, and prayed. But it does mean that all of our private, lonely prayers are to be seen as linked with those of our community. Even alone we are communal, and never more so than when we are praying the psalms, for then we are joining the community of an ancient king who himself was a member of the community of the King.

It makes no difference which of the psalms might be the product of an individual psalmist such as David. All of them were set in the context of a community. They are as relevant for twenty-first-century Christians as for the ancient Hebrew nation. They fit our needs as our own answering speech. We can see how this is so with Psalm 32.

THE LEADER

For a psalm to be prayed in community, a leader will be necessary. The best leaders will be those who have already studied the psalm and have prayed it for themselves. The deeper the leader's grasp of the psalm, the wiser will be the leadership, for some on-the-spot adaptation will probably be necessary to fit the circumstance.

The following guide assumes familiarity with the present chapter. First comes a small group study guide designed to be used by the leader, followed by a guided prayer in which each member is invited to pray silently and occasionally aloud together with specific words.

Small Group Study of Psalm 32

The following comments are directed to the leader.

Introduction

Introduce the group to the concept of praying through the psalms by briefly summarizing your own experience of praying Psalm 32. Don't mention any of the details of the psalm itself, its content or its ultimate aim. Just describe the general idea. Then lead the group into the psalm by asking the following questions.

Group Questions

1. Have one person read Psalm 32 in its entirety at an ordinary pace.

2. Have another person read it very slowly, with a pause after each verse.

3. A third reading would be appropriate—but not if it looks as if people in the group are getting restless.

4. What is the main topic of the psalm?

5. Summarize the flow of ideas in the psalm. (If this is found difficult, refer to the section on rational structure earlier in this chapter.) Then focus on the details by asking the following questions.

6. Who is happy? Who is unhappy? Why? (See vv. 1-4.)

(The following questions could prove awkward, embarrassing or too personal for some in the group to answer. So stress that you and the group do not have any interest—morbid or otherwise—in learning what sins are being recalled. This study is not designed to create a "confessional" in which you as leader or the group as a community provide forgiveness or absolution of guilt. Only God can forgive sins against God or even sins against others, for these sins are also sins against God. You are trying to get each person to focus on his or her own past, its troubles and its violations of God's design for us.)

7. Drawing on your own experience of guilt over sin, do you find the imagery too extreme or not extreme enough? Explain.

8. How does verse 5 reflect your experience? (Some may wish to recount their conversion experience. If they do, encourage them to keep it short. Then ask them if they have ever felt a need for confession of new sins.)

9. What encouragement do verses 6-7 give those who repent?

   What attitude does heaven itself have toward the repentance of sinners? (You could refer to Luke 15:7.)

10. Look at how God instructs his children in verses 8-9. What is your reaction to being likened to a horse or mule?

    What images reflect your own experience of rebellion against God?

11. Trace the emotional flow in the psalm from happiness to joy. (See earlier in this chapter, pp. 23-24, if help is needed for this.)

12. What should be our response to God's forgiveness and our restoration to peace with him (v. 11)?

    Does this response seem reasonable or appropriate to you?

DIRECTED PRAYER

The following can act as a script for the directed prayer.
Leader: Let us pray through Psalm 32. (You as leader read the psalm and direct the group.)

   [1]Happy are those whose transgression is forgiven,

whose sin is covered.
²Happy are those to whom the LORD imputes no iniquity,
　　and in whose spirit there is no deceit.

Leader: Reflect silently on what is required for happiness before God.
　(Pause.)

³While I kept silence, my body wasted away
　　through my groaning all day long.
⁴For day and night your hand was heavy upon me;
　　my strength dried up as by the heat of summer.

　　　　　　　　　　　　　　　　　　　　Selah

Leader: Remember your experience with God as you realized the depths of
your sins and your strong propensity for continuing in them.
　(Pause.)

⁵Then I acknowledged my sin to you,
　　and I did not hide my iniquity;
　I said, "I will confess my transgressions to the LORD" . . .

　　　　　　　　　　　　　　　　　　　　Selah

Leader: Now silently confess those sins which have sprung to mind, especially those that are the most troublesome (pause),
　those you keep committing though you know you should not (pause),
　those that are recent and not really fully acknowledged (longer pause).

　. . . And you forgave the guilt of my sin.

Let the fact of God's forgiveness sink deep in your consciousness.
　(Pause.)

⁶Therefore let all who are faithful

offer prayer to you;
at a time of distress, the rush of mighty waters
shall not reach them.
⁷You are a hiding place for me;
you preserve me from trouble;
you surround me with glad cries of deliverance.

Selah

Leader: I invite several of you to pray aloud for strength to live lives worthy of God's call to you.

(Pause. You may wish to model such a prayer in a *few* words. This time of public prayer is for the group members to solidify their commitment.)

⁸I will instruct you and teach you the way you should go;
I will counsel you with my eye upon you.
⁹Do not be like a horse or a mule, without understanding,
whose temper must be curbed with bit and bridle,
else it will not stay near you.

Leader: Thank God for his counsel, for reminding you of what you probably already know. And pray silently for the spiritual stamina to sustain your side of your relationship with God.

(Pause.)

¹⁰Many are the torments of the wicked,
but steadfast love surrounds those who trust in the LORD.
¹¹Be glad in the LORD and rejoice, O righteous,
and shout for joy, all you upright in heart.

(Sing together a hymn or a praise song—one that will be known by most of the group.)

Leader: (as a closing to your time together) And all the people said:
Group members: Amen!

PARTING WORDS

There is no way to tell what the experience of each of the participants will have been at the end of such a session. Invite participants to talk with each other about some of what they have learned and felt—about God, themselves, prayer, the psalm itself.

Waiting for the Lord
Psalm 130

Discouragement, disappointment, even despair—these are common to of all of us. For some the sense of abandonment is severe and seemingly endless. For others it is less frequent, less intense and less long lasting. But there are times when everyone can only cry out from the depths.

The French poet Charles-Pierre Baudelaire caught the spirit of such despair in his poem based on the theme of Psalm 130. "The skies are lead," he writes. There's no horizon. "I share this night with blasphemy and dread." Throughout his poem the bitter gloom of Baudelaire is unrelieved. But not so the gloom of the ancient psalmist: here is his cry from the depths amidst his firm hope for relief.

INITIAL READING OF PSALM 130

Psalm 130 (NIV)

A song of ascents

¹Out of the depths I cry to you, O LORD;
²   O Lord, hear my voice.
Let your ears be attentive
    to my cry for mercy.

³If you, O LORD, kept a record of sins,
   O Lord, who could stand?
⁴But with you there is forgiveness;
   therefore you are feared.

⁵I wait for the LORD, my soul waits,
   and in his word I put my hope.
⁶My soul waits for the Lord
   more than watchmen wait for the morning,
   more than watchmen wait for the morning.

⁷O Israel, put your hope in the LORD,
   for with the LORD is unfailing love
   and with him is full redemption.
⁸He himself will redeem Israel
   from all their sins.

When we approach any psalm to make its words our "answering speech" to God, we must grasp it well enough for our thoughts to parallel those of the psalmist. So I will repeat the instructions given in the previous chapter. Read the psalm again more slowly. Then once again. Read it until the words seep easily into your conscious mind. With each reading, observe and absorb the words and sentences, the images and ideas. Do this with a completely open mind, without prejudging what the psalmist is concerned for.

GETTING AT THE MEANING OF PSALM 130

In our reading, have we sensed the profound longing of the psalmist? If not, perhaps we will do so as we look at the words and the rational, emotional and rhetorical structures.

The Meaning of the Words

We begin with individual words. Some of them have surely popped out as interesting and significant. Some are especially intriguing. The very first line, for instance, contains a striking phrase: *out of the depths.*

For the psalmist "the deep," the sea or ocean, is a primal force of chaos; God has created and ordered it, but it still threatens to undo humankind. When the psalmist calls from *the depths*, then, he is calling from a place of danger with a fear of being overwhelmed, in particular from the chaos of the sins that encompass him.

The sheer multiple repetition of two other words within the short psalm is also striking. Four times the psalmist addresses God: O LORD (Yahweh) or O Lord (Adonai). The psalm arises out of the psalmist's agony, but it focuses quickly and with determination on God, who will deliver. The second word is *wait*, repeated four times. The concept itself is at the center of the psalm, the link between discouragement and deliverance.

Finally the repeated phrase *more than watchmen wait for the morning* stands out. In ancient times, and still today in communities troubled by violence, watchmen keep vigil throughout the night. Long hours of standing, walking and sleepless sitting characterize their night. Many years ago, as officer of the guard aboard a troop ship bound to Asia in peacetime, I found a guard sleeping. I should probably just have chewed him out, but I wrote him up and was the witness at a summary court-martial aboard the ship. His punishment was mild; the military judge docked his pay. A watchman who falls asleep in time of war is not treated quite so casually.

The psalmist, however, does not emphasize the imminent danger of his job so much as the desire for morning. *Wait* is another word for *hope*, a looking forward to the time when the watchman can be relieved. In the darkness of his soul, the watchman yearns for light.

Overall Rational Structure

A cry to the Lord from the depths

¹Out of the depths I cry to you, O LORD;
²   O Lord, hear my voice.
Let your ears be attentive
     to my cry for mercy.

The Lord who forgives

³If you, O LORD, kept a record of sins,
     O Lord, who could stand?
⁴But with you there is forgiveness;
     therefore you are feared.

Waiting for the Lord

⁵I wait for the LORD, my soul waits,
     and in his word I put my hope.
⁶My soul waits for the Lord
     more than watchmen wait for the morning,
     more than watchmen wait for the morning.

Israel's hope in the Lord

⁷O Israel, put your hope in the LORD,
     for with the LORD is unfailing love
     and with him is full redemption.
⁸He himself will redeem Israel
     from all their sins.

The structure of ideas is clear. (1) The psalmist in his individual anguish calls out to God for relief from the guilt of his sin. (2) He states the reason for his confidence: his utter reliance on the mercy of God, who is to be feared. (3) He waits in hope for God's deliverance. (4) He stands aside from his own situation and calls on all Israel to put their hope in God. Let us look at each of these sections in turn.

First, the psalmist knows he has a long record of sin, but his grasp of God's forgiveness is firm. Still, God is not to be treated as a cosmic grandfather who can be counted on simply to look the other way. His very forgiving character is backed by his awesome greatness, so that even in his forgiveness he is to be feared.

Second, the God of the Bible is no tribal deity to be placated by rituals and animal sacrifices. Nor is he one simply to accept worship on one day a week, do what you like on the rest. He is, rather, an awesome God. When Moses sought the face of God, God told him he would die if he were to grant Moses' request. Then God proclaimed this paradoxical word:

> The LORD, the LORD,
> a God merciful and gracious,
> slow to anger,
> keeping steadfast love for the thousandth generation,
> forgiving iniquity and transgression and sin,
> yet by no means clearing the guilty,
> but visiting the iniquity of the parents
> upon the children
> and the children's children,
> to the third and the fourth generation. (Ex 34:6-7)

No wonder Moses responded as he did: "And Moses quickly bowed his head toward the earth, and worshiped. He said, 'If now I have found favor in your sight, O Lord, I pray, let the Lord go with us. Although this is a stiff-necked people, pardon our iniquity and our sin, and take us for your inheritance'" (Ex 34:8-9).

This paradox—a loving God who punishes the guilty—is not resolved until God comes in human form and shows us that he himself takes on the guilt of our sin and dies in our place. Moses and the psalmist could only look forward in hope. We can look both backward and forward—backward first to hear what Moses was told, then to hear what Jesus told us and showed us, then forward to what we know from Jesus' words about the future. "In my Father's house," he said, "there are many dwelling places. If it were not so, would I have told you that I go to prepare a place for you? . . . I will come again and will take you to myself, so that where I am, there you may be also" (Jn 14:2-3). Here is compassion and love.

Still, Jesus warned us: "God is spirit, and those who worship him must worship in spirit and in truth" (Jn 4:24). The proper response from us is awed wonder and fear—and not the sort of fear that comes when we face one who would merely take our life. No, Jesus said that we are to "fear him who, after he has killed, has authority to cast into hell" (Lk 12:5). This terrifying-loving God, then, is the Lord of the repeated *O Lords.*

Third, the psalmist waits for God's response. This may be the most difficult part of the psalm to realize as our answering speech, for this particular speech calls us to wait—to stop flailing our inner arms, even to stop praying our endless prattling prayers, to be still, to remain silent as we are. We are such a wordy people. Our waking mind is stuffed full of chatter. Even in our private consciousness, silence is conspicuous by its absence. In the outer world it's no better. Even now in my den, with the windows closed and neither radio nor TV, LP nor CD, tape or DVD blathering in the background, I hear a long freight train rattling along the Burlington-Northern tracks toward Chicago.

But the psalmist has addressed our need. He has repeated the phrase

more than watchmen wait for the morning,
more than watchmen wait for the morning.

Our attention is doubly drawn to waiting. We may remember the final doubled lines of Robert Frost's famous poem: "and miles to go before I sleep." We hear more in these lines than a mere echo: something mysterious is going on in this poem. So too in Psalm 130, something mysterious is going on. The psalmist's longing for the morning is as intense as was his sense of anguish in the opening line. What are we to learn from this?

During the few months of my sabbatical a few years ago, I learned at least some of the value of silence. Each morning I would drive to a nearby woods, have my devotions from the Bible and a guide book, and then, because there was rarely enough material to take up the full hour I had set aside for devotions, I would simply wait in silence, wait for what I had read to sink in. There were only a few verses of Scripture and a few comments by spiritually wise men and women. But this was enough. Sometimes a sense of God's presence emerged in the silence. Sometimes I would try to picture Jesus walking toward me from under the beautiful bough of a tree some fifty yards away. He never came. But I waited. These devotional sessions triggered some of my richest spiritual experiences. I came to know that Christ was there—visible or not. I knew, as Julian of Norwich knew, that

All will be well,
And all will be well.
And all manner of thing will be well.

Waiting is not having. It is hoping. It is knowing in your heart of hearts that what we have committed to God will be kept by him for realization in his good time. We may groan inwardly now, we may cry from the depths, but see with the heart of faith: "For in hope we were saved. Now hope that is seen is not hope. For who hopes for what is seen? But if we hope for what we do not see, we wait for it with patience" (Rom 8:24-25).

Václav Havel, though not writing from a Christian perspective, understands this kind of hope: "Either we have hope in us or we don't; it is a dimension of the soul, and it's not essentially dependent on some particular observation of the world or estimate of the situation. Hope is not prognostication. It is an orientation of the spirit, an orientation of the heart; it transcends the world that is immediately experienced, and is anchored somewhere beyond its horizons."

The anchor of hope is indeed beyond the horizons of hope. The anchor of hope is in God, the God who speaks, the God who comes. "In his word I put my hope," says the psalmist. Surely this would include the words of Moses and other of God's prophets. There is a substantial revelation on which the psalmist relies.

With the coming of Christ, we too have such a word—an even more substantial word. We need not be like Estragon and Vladimir in Samuel Beckett's *Waiting for Godot;* they play absurd word games as they wait for Godot—a man, a god?—who never comes. In Jesus Christ, God has come. In his brilliant Word he speaks truth to us. As the Holy Spirit, God lives in us. So we wait in a hope that daily, hourly and minute by minute is being realized. We are saved, being saved and yet to be saved.

The psalmist, centuries earlier in the salvation history of humankind, redirects us to this realization by calling us, when we cry out to God, to wait for him even more than a watchman waits for the morning. In this call the ancient psalmist is a thousand times more relevant than the psychologist with the latest therapy.

Fourth and finally, the psalmist turns outward to his compatriots and calls on them to put their hope in God. For God's forgiveness extends to all his people, not just to a special brand of prophet, poet, priest or saint. God's love is unfailing. His redemption is full. Israel and all of us are in his hands.

Emotional Structure

We have already seen much of the emotional structure in our analysis of the rational structure. But it will help to summarize it:

- agony (v. 1)
- pleading (v. 2)
- amazement at the character of God (vv. 3-4)
- fear of God (v. 4)
- quiet longing (vv. 5-6)
- confident faith (vv. 7-8)

Psalm 130 takes us from the depths (vv. 1-2) to the heights (vv. 3-4) and back down to the world of ordinary individual life (vv. 5-6) and corporate life (vv. 7-8).

Rhetorical Structure

There is one more element of this psalm that we can benefit from considering before we proceed to make it our answering speech. Hebrew poetry has some features that are rare or even largely foreign to English literature. It was rare, for example, for American poets before Walt Whitman to build on parallel structures. In many—I am tempted to say most—of the psalms, this structure is systemic. Recall, for example, these verses from Psalm 32:

[1]Happy are those whose transgression is forgiven,
   whose sin is covered.
[2]Happy are those to whom the LORD imputes no iniquity,
   and in whose spirit there is no deceit.

The ideas in the first line are repeated, though the words are changed. Or notice these lines from the same psalm:

[7]You are a hiding place for me;
   you preserve me from trouble;
   you surround me with glad cries of deliverance.

Here each succeeding line adds content to the first line. Another frequent form is antithesis. The closing lines of Psalm 32 illustrate both antithetical and supportive forms:

[10]Many are the torments of the wicked,
   but steadfast love surrounds those who trust in the LORD.
[11]Be glad in the LORD and rejoice, O righteous,
   and shout for joy, all you upright in heart.

Because parallel forms are so common in the psalms, there is little special significance to any one of them. They do, of course, reinforce the ideas and place emphasis on the important concepts, but they are so ordinary that most of them have no special force.

In Psalm 130 various parallel forms are found in verses 1, 3-4, 5, 5-6 and 7. But the most interesting of them is found in verse 6, where the second line is identical to the first.

[6]My soul waits for the Lord
   more than watchmen wait for the morning,
   more than watchmen wait for the morning.

This form of repetition is rare in the psalms. I think that indicates it has a special role in this psalm. Here, the psalmist is saying, is a very important idea. It is indeed the center of the psalmist's response to God. In effect and in brief, he is saying, "O Lord, you are my salvation. I wait for you!"

This conclusion is supported by a second consideration. One form often found in Hebrew poetry is not used in modern poetry. This is the chiastic structure. Here the context of the key idea comes first, then the key idea, then the context again. Look at verse 6 in the context of verses 5 and 7:

> ⁵I wait for the LORD, my soul waits,
>> and in his word I put my hope.
> ⁶My soul waits for the Lord
>> more than watchmen wait for the morning,
>> more than watchmen wait for the morning.
>
> ⁷O Israel, put your hope in the LORD,
>> for with the LORD is unfailing love
>> and with him is full redemption.

The pattern here is a a b a a a b: that is *wait, wait, hope, wait, wait, wait, hope.* The pattern is not perfect, for the word *wait* occurs twice before the word *hope,* but the chiastic structure is there nonetheless.

So what should we conclude about the contribution of aesthetic form to the meaning of the psalm? Just this: Among the several notions in the psalm, *waiting for God* is one of the most important. Conceptually, emotionally and aesthetically the psalm is all of a piece—a single unit, a little gem of spiritual wisdom. It should be a joy to make it our answering speech.

PRAYING PSALM 130

Read through the entire psalm again. Then with eyes open, read and pray
section by section:

> ¹Out of the depths I cry to you, O LORD;
> ²   O Lord, hear my voice.
> Let your ears be attentive
>   to my cry for mercy.

Respond by assessing where you feel you stand with God. If you are in
the depths as was the psalmist, then you may pray these lines with full
accord. If you are not, tell God where you feel you are. If you fail to feel
that you really need God and his forgiveness, then you are not ready to
pray this psalm. Spend some time reading Romans 3; then continue with
praying the psalm.

Say to God: *O Lord, I cry to you from deep within me. Here is how I feel.* Tell
God what you have learned in assessing your spiritual condition.

> ³If you, O LORD, kept a record of sins,
>   O Lord, who could stand?

Respond: *Lord, there is no one who stands blameless before you. Is there even any other
person whose sins are more than mine? It doesn't matter. My sins alone are enough to send
you to the cross.*

> ⁴But with you there is forgiveness;
>   therefore you are feared.

Respond: *Thank you for your great mercy! And in my joy over your forgiveness, let me
always realize that I stand before a holy God—a forgiving God but one who judges.*
Pause to meditate on the complex compassionate and stern character of
God.

⁵I wait for the LORD, my soul waits,
    and in his word I put my hope.

Respond: Wait for a few moments in the presence of God, pondering the fact that God in his Word, specifically the word of this psalm, is trustworthy. Then pray: *Thank you, Lord, for giving your people a word that is faithful and true, a word we can trust, a word that tells us what we should hope for and why!*

⁶My soul waits for the Lord
    more than watchmen wait for the morning,
    more than watchmen wait for the morning.

Respond: Here, in perhaps the most difficult part of the psalm to pray, simply wait. Keep silent for as long as you can, then longer. Remember that from our human point of view, this is the center of the psalm. It is in silence that the center of reality can and will be present with you. Wait in hope—a hope that is being realized though you may not always realize it, a hope in the abiding presence of the living Lord of the universe, the One who has everything under his control. Expect his presence, but do not expect an extraordinary experience such as a vision or an emotional jolt. God usually shows up in quiet ways. In silence he works his way with our heart. The proof is not in the immediate experience but in the quiet sense of the rightness of our relationship with God, a sense that persists in the ordinary course of life. So wait.

When the waiting is over and the Spirit moves you to continue, say these final verses with confidence as a prayer for your community, your church, your country, your world.

⁷O Israel, put your hope in the LORD,
    for with the LORD is unfailing love
    and with him is full redemption.

[8]He himself will redeem Israel
    from all their sins.

SOME FURTHER REFLECTIONS

This prayer is not for praying just once. It can well become one of the central psalms in your spiritual development. Pray it often. And when you can make the opportunity, lead others to pray the prayer with you.

Small Group Study of Psalm 130

The following comments are directed to the leader.

Introduction

Introduce this psalm by briefly telling the group about its impact on you when you have prayed it. Don't give away the meaning of the psalm in your introduction. Let the participants come to see this for themselves. You may well learn from them as the study proceeds.

Group Instructions and Questions

1. Have one person read Psalm 130 in its entirety at an ordinary pace.

2. Have another person read it very slowly, with a pause after each verse.

3. A third reading would be appropriate—but not if it looks as if people in the group are getting restless.

4. Have the participants outline the main sections of the psalm (see p. 39) so that they grasp the flow of ideas.

5. In what frame of mind does the psalmist begin?

    What troubles him more than anything else?

6. How does the psalmist express his grasp of the sinfulness of sin? (If there are those who do not understand the universality of sin among us, direct attention to such Scriptures as Romans 3:9-18, 23; James 1:12-15; I John 1:8-10.)

7. Notice that the dual character of God is mentioned in verse 4. Why do you think the psalmist sees "fear" of God as the logical response to God's forgiveness?

    How can mercy and holiness both be characteristic of God?

8. Why is the phrase "more than watchmen wait for the morning" repeated?

   Why do you think the psalmist "waits" for the Lord?

9. What does waiting involve? (The leader may wish to comment on the character of waiting, hoping and silence, using some of the ideas on pages 40-41.)

10. Why do you think the psalmist shifts his attention in the final two verses?

11. In preparation for the directed prayer, summarize the emotional flow of the psalm.

DIRECTED PRAYER

The following script may help the group to pray the psalm.

Leader: Let us pray through Psalm 130. Please realize that this prayer will include at least one long period of silence. Let us read together the first two verses. (The leader and the group read verses 1-2.)

¹Out of the depths I cry to you, O LORD;
²   O Lord, hear my voice.
   Let your ears be attentive
      to my cry for mercy.

Leader: We pause now for a few moments. Open your heart before God. Tell God where you think you are in your relationship with him. Then in silence cry out to him and lay before him your burden of sin or sadness or troubles. Ask for his mercy.

(Pause for at least two minutes; then read for the group the following verses. The group will not read together till the final verses.)

³If you, O LORD, kept a record of sins,
O Lord, who could stand?

Consider the vast gulf between all of us and God due to our sin. (Pause.)

⁴But with you there is forgiveness;
therefore you are feared.

(Pause.)

Consider the glorious paradox of forgiveness sparking fear, and the glorious paradox of fear in which there is hope.

⁵I wait for the LORD, my soul waits,
and.in his word I put my hope.
⁶My soul waits for the Lord
more than watchmen wait for the morning,
more than watchmen wait for the morning.

Let us wait in silence. As watchmen throughout a long night anticipate the certainty of the morning's coming, let us anticipate the certainty of God's presence with us. Let us keep watch.

(Pause. The leader must use good judgment for how long. Five to ten minutes may be appropriate. Some may wish to go longer, especially where there is little to disturb the silence. The leader then breaks silence.)

In the presence of God, let us say together the final two verses of the psalm.

⁷O Israel, put your hope in the LORD,
for with the LORD is unfailing love
and with him is full redemption.
⁸He himself will redeem Israel
from all their sins.

May we with boldness display before our friends, neighbors and fellow workers the unfailing love of God and call them to place their trust in the Lord, ask God for forgiveness and place their lives in his hands. For God himself will redeem not only Israel but all those who call on his name.

PARTING REMARKS

Praying intently in a group may bring all sorts of responses from participants. Leaders should listen carefully to their comments. Some may have profoundly personal and intimate experiences. Some of these may well be shared with the group. Others may best be recounted only in one-on-one conversation. So try to be sensitive to the situation and, as host, use good judgment about whether to encourage people to talk about their experience in the group.

Night Thoughts
Psalm 4

Rejoice always, pray without ceasing, give thanks in all circumstances; for this is the will of God in Christ Jesus for you," the apostle Paul told the Thessalonians (1 Thess 5:16-18). Just three short commands. But look at them: Rejoice . . . pray . . . give thanks. Do these always. Three impossible demands. What a high call for the Thessalonians!

Shouldn't all of us as Christians strive to follow Paul's call? But just how? The answer is clear: step by step, day by day; each step coming closer, each day a bit further, till one day beyond the veil of days, the will of God for us is realized. Meanwhile, we soldier on.

Perhaps the rejoicing and the thanking will be easier when we do the praying. Psalm 4, designed for a particular time of day, will be a good place to begin.

INITIAL READING OF PSALM 4

Psalm 4
To the leader: with stringed instruments.
A Psalm of David.

¹Answer me when I call, O God of my right!

You gave me room when I was in distress.
Be gracious to me, and hear my prayer.

[2]How long, you people, shall my honor suffer shame?
How long will you love vain words, and seek after lies?

Selah

[3]But know that the LORD has set apart the faithful for himself;
the LORD hears when I call to him.

[4]When you are disturbed, do not sin;
ponder it on your beds, and be silent.   *Selah*
[5]Offer right sacrifices,
and put your trust in the LORD.

[6]There are many who say, "O that we might see some good!
Let the light of your face shine on us, O LORD!"
[7]You have put gladness in my heart
more than when their grain and wine abound.

[8]I will both lie down and sleep in peace;
for you alone, O LORD, make me lie down in safety.

Read and reread this psalm slowly until you not only intellectually understand but feel in your soul that you have absorbed the words and ideas.

GETTING AT THE MEANING OF PSALM 4

Remember that even after you feel you have grasped the psalm through slow, careful reading, you may change your mind about what it means as you study it in the light of biblical scholarship and further intellectual reflection.

Rational Structure

This psalm has clear subject breaks between the various stanzas, but, as may already be clear, it has the structure of a reverie more than that of a rational argument. It is like a conversation one might have with oneself upon retiring for the night. In short, it is a reverie about a reverie.

Invocation and prayer

¹Answer me when I call, O God of my right!

> You gave me room when I was in distress.
> Be gracious to me, and hear my prayer.

The context of his plea

²How long, you people, shall my honor suffer shame?

> How long will you love vain words, and seek after lies?
>
> *Selah*

Confirmation of confidence

³But know that the LORD has set apart the faithful for himself;

> the LORD hears when I call to him.

Advice to oneself and others

⁴When you are disturbed, do not sin;

> ponder it on your beds, and be silent.   *Selah*

⁵Offer right sacrifices,

> and put your trust in the LORD.

The desire for God's presence

⁶There are many who say, "O that we might see some good!

> Let the light of your face shine on us, O LORD!"

The beneficence of God

⁷You have put gladness in my heart
  more than when their grain and wine abound.

Final confidence in God

⁸I will both lie down and sleep in peace;
  for you alone, O LORD, make me lie down in safety.

This psalm, like Psalm 32, is universally human. It applies as much to our age as to that of the psalmist. This fact has not been lost on the church, for the psalm has been found ideal for evening contemplation for centuries. "Psalm 4 has always been a prayer for the hour when the onset of darkness brings the day to its close," writes Stanley Jaki. "In the old Roman Breviary this psalm was part of each Sunday Completorium. In monasteries that follow the Rule of St. Benedict this psalm was sung every evening as the monks gathered for the canonical Hour [compline]." We change little as human beings. What led the psalmist to create this little gem of prayer is echoed in the hearts of us all.

The context is easy for us to imagine: The psalmist is preparing to retire. He has come to the end of a long day; thoughts of God have flitted in and out of his consciousness; his daily routines have been disturbed by countless interruptions. Worse, he has been hassled by people who are maligning him, obstructing his goals, bringing down shame on him. He is dog tired and he needs relief. So he falls on his knees and cries out to God—not just any God with any character, but *God of my right*, that is, God who knows the psalmist is right and does not deserve the carping of critics. *Be gracious to me,* he pleads, *and hear my prayer.*

Then his mind turns away from God to his critics and enemies. *How long?* he cries. Over sixty times the phrase *how long* leaps out of Scripture.

Sometimes it is the psalmist or some other individual asking how long God will suffer them to suffer. Sometimes it is God lamenting the failures of his people who suffer him to suffer. *How long* is a strong emotional phrase. It doesn't just ask a question that can be answered with a calendar date. It expresses a deep longing for relief.

The psalmist does not linger over his frustration. He knows this is not necessary, for he knows who God is and what he does for those who are faithful to him. The Lord will hear, he assures himself: *But know that the LORD has set apart the faithful for himself; the LORD hears when I call to him* (v. 3). In fact, before he has even made his plea for God to hear, he reminds God that he had relieved his stress before: *You gave me room* [some translations say *relief*] *when I was in distress* (v. 1). There is, in other words, a seesaw structure to these first three verses:

Plea	**Confidence in God**
1a, answer me	1b, you gave me room
1c, be gracious to me	
2, lament against enemies	3, the LORD hears

Back and forth goes the psalmist's mind as he seeks peace of mind and remembers its earlier presence. Then he thinks: what should we do when we are disturbed? Obvious: we should ponder our situation, know it for what it is. Bedtime, just before settling down to sleep, is a good time for this. George Swinock (1627-1673) has a few wise words on pondering on our bed:

Secrecy is the best opportunity for this duty. The silent night is a good time for this speech. When we have no outward objects to disturb us, and to call our eyes, as the fool's eyes are always, to the ends of the earth; then our eyes, as the eyes of the wise, may be broad inwards. The most successful searches have been made in the night

season; the soul is then wholly shut up in the earthly house of the
body, and hath no visits from strangers to disquiet its thoughts.

As we ponder, we should not gloss over any reality that we have been
wronged by others. But when we have recognized this, we should forget
it. We should not lash out but be silent.

My grandfather used to counsel me, when I got upset over something
I thought unfair: "Shake your fist in your pocket, boy. Shake your fist in
your pocket." The apostle Paul may well have had Psalm 4 in mind when
he wrote to the Ephesians, "Be angry but do not sin; do not let the sun go
down on your anger" (4:26). So there the psalmist is, in his bed, recalling
the struggles of the day, whose roots lie in fallen human nature. He ponders the situation and then stops. He turns off the internal chatter and
keeps silence. Silence, you will recall, is also the center of Psalm 130.

But there is also more that can be done. The psalmist realizes that he
can "offer right sacrifices" and "trust in the LORD." For him this means
keeping the ongoing rites of the synagogue or the temple, being regular
at worship. But it means more than this, as David in his profound penitential prayer, Psalm 51, says:

> [17]The sacrifice acceptable to God is a broken spirit;
>   a broken and contrite heart, O God, you will not despise.

The prophet Micah insists that what God really wants is not "thousands of rams" or "ten thousand rivers of oil." Rather, the Lord requires
the psalmist "to do justice, and to love kindness, and to walk humbly
with your God" (Micah 6:7-8).

For us there is no question of animal sacrifice. Jesus has atoned for all
our sin. Our sacrifice is simply our service as his followers, to act as he acted,
to imitate Christ. "I appeal to you therefore, brothers and sisters," writes
Paul, "by the mercies of God, to present your bodies as a living sacrifice,

holy and acceptable to God, which is your spiritual worship" (Rom 12:1).

After silence, after waiting, the psalmist's mind is again at work as he reflects on his and others' desire for good things to happen, but not to receive only material blessings. What he and others really want is the very presence of God. The psalmist here is imitating Moses, who, up on the mountain and alone, called out to the great I AM, "Show me your glory" (Ex 33:18).

Though God does not respond to the psalmist with an awesome word of revelation, he does act. For between verses 6 and 7, the Lord responds: the psalmist acknowledges that God has *put gladness* in his heart, more inner, spiritual gladness than those who have troubled him have when their crops are good. His gladness is better than the gladness of the most glorious wine.

It is only after this intimate dialogue with God that the psalmist can relax. Now, however, he can do so with great confidence and relief. His final words are magnificent and fitting: *I will both lie down and sleep in peace,* he says, dividing the conscious from the unconscious, but finding peace in both and giving honor to the *God of my right* who has answered his call.

Emotional Structure

When we single out the emotional from the rational, we can summarize the structure this way:

- urgent distress and frustration (v. 1)
- hope for resolution (v. 1)
- longing for relief (v. 2)
- intellectual confidence in God (v. 3)
- calm practice of emotional discipline (v. 4)
- calm acknowledgment of right religious attitudes and practices (v. 5)
- calm, earnest turning to God (v. 6)

- joy in God's answer (v. 7)
- deep sense of physical, emotional and spiritual peace (v. 8)

The psalm, then, moves from frustration to resolution, tension to release, antagonism to peace. It should be a joy for us to make it our answering speech. And doing so should also lead us to "rejoice always, pray without ceasing, [and] give thanks in all circumstances" much more readily (I Thess 5:16-18).

PRAYING PSALM 4

Read through the entire psalm again. Then, with eyes open, read and pray section by section. These instructions assume that this will be an evening prayer, but it is certainly not inappropriate for other times in the day. In any case, the instructions below can easily be adapted to fit the situation.

> ¹Answer me when I call, O God of my right!
>> You gave me room when I was in distress.
>> Be gracious to me, and hear my prayer.

Respond: *O Lord, here I am again at the end of the day, feeling not just tired in body but tired in soul and spirit. You are the God of my right. You know my heart. Search me. I believe that much of my trouble and sorrow is coming from outside me. I believe I am living the way you want me to—at least most of the time. Forgive me when I fail. But hear me when I tell you what really troubles me.* Now pour out your specific concerns to God. You are alone before him. Give details. Name names. Be honest about how you feel. Then continue to pray the psalm.

> ²How long, you people, shall my honor suffer shame?
>> How long will you love vain words, and seek after lies?
>>> *Selah*

Respond: Pour out to God your feelings about the injustice you and others are experiencing. Then continue to pray the psalm.

> [3]But know that the LORD has set apart the faithful for himself;
>   the LORD hears when I call to him.

Respond: *Lord, I know who you are—at least something of who you are. I know you have set apart the faithful for yourself. I trust you. You have delivered me before. After the captivity of Israel in Egypt were the exodus and the Promised Land. After the exile in Babylon were the return to Jerusalem and the building of the temple. After the crucifixion was the resurrection. You have heard when I have called. You will hear now.*

> [4]When you are disturbed, do not sin;
>   ponder it on your beds, and be silent.   *Selah*

Respond: Ponder now. Cast your mind back on your situation, wrestle with your feelings, but ease off the tension. Don't lash out at your "enemies" or the troubling circumstances that have brought frustration. Pepper your pondering with periods of silence. Stop your inner chatter. Wait before the Lord. Then continue. Tell yourself:

> [5]Offer right sacrifices,
>   and put your trust in the LORD.

Respond: *Lord, there is much that I can do to ease my situation. I can offer some right sacrifices.* Tell the Lord your intentions for worship and for fresh a start in honoring God with your life, doing justice, loving kindness and walking humbly with God.

> [6]There are many who say, "O that we might see some good!
>   Let the light of your face shine on us, O LORD!"

Respond: *Lord, I long to see justice and mercy for myself, yes, but also for others. I bring before you those who I know cry out for your goodness.* Name sufferers whom you know; bring before God people who are oppressed by evil regimes or besieged by terrorism. Meditate on their plight and pray for them by name if you can. *Come Lord Jesus, shed your light on us, illumine my heart. Show me how I can show mercy.*

Pause in inner silence.

[7]You have put gladness in my heart
    more than when their grain and wine abound.

Respond: *Thank you, Lord, for showing me you care, you hear and answer prayer.* If in praying you have experienced the presence of God in your heart and soul, tell him so.

[8]I will both lie down and sleep in peace;
    for you alone, O LORD, make me lie down in safety.

Respond: *I now rest my spirit in you. I lie down. May my sleep be sound, undisturbed by troubling dreams. May I rise in the morning with abundant energy and determination to live the day for you! Amen.*

SOME FURTHER REFLECTIONS

One of the joys of disciplined prayer is repetition. This prayer can be used every night for a week or more as the preface to your night's sleep. Contrary to expectation, rather than becoming boring, it is likely to command more and more of your attention and thus lead more and more to your saying to God, *You have put gladness in my heart.*

Small Group Study of Psalm 4

The following comments are directed to the leader.

Introduction

This psalm is deeply intimate and personal. It seems to have been intended for individual prayer. But the church has always seen it to be just as relevant for groups. Explain this to the participants, then lead them in a discussion.

Group Instructions and Questions

1. Have one person read Psalm 4 in its entirety at an ordinary pace.

2. Have another person read it very slowly, with a pause after each verse.

3. A third reading would be appropriate—but not if it looks as if people in the group are getting restless.

4. How might praying this psalm at night be helpful?

5. With what attitude does the psalmist begin (vv. 1-2)?

   What hope does he have from the beginning that God might hear him (v. 1)?

6. Have someone read the psalm again, and ask participants to notice the shifts in the psalmist's emotions. Then ask someone to trace them briefly. (The answer should reflect the gist of the emotional structure, outlined on pp. 60-61.) How does this structure reflect the character of your own inner dialogue before sleep?

7. What does the psalmist seem most concerned about (v. 2)?

   What situations today might be similar to those the psalmist faced?

8. Why do you think the psalmist in verse 3 is confident of an answer to his plea?

9. Explain the advice given in verse 5.

   Do you think it's a good response to the problem the psalmist faces?

   What wider application might it have beyond the situation assumed in the psalm (see Eph 4:26)? Explain.

10. What kind of ongoing sacrifices does God now require of his children?

    What light is shed on this question by Psalm 51:16-17, Micah 6:8 and Romans 12:1?

11. After his request in verse 6, why does the psalmist consider himself in a better situation than that of his prosperous enemies?

12. What is the psalmist's physical, spiritual and emotional condition at the end of the psalm?

DIRECTED PRAYER

The following script may help the group to pray the psalm.

Leader: Let us pray through Psalm 4. Though we will not be going to bed directly after we meditate on this psalm, may we find ourselves ready to receive the peace of God in our lives now. Let's say the first verse together:

> ¹Answer me when I call, O God of my right!
>> You gave me room when I was in distress.
>> Be gracious to me, and hear my prayer.

Leader: We have called on God to attend to our besieged condition. Now let us contemplate our specific situation:

> ²How long, you people, shall my honor suffer shame?

How long will you love vain words, and seek after lies?

Selah

Leader: Call to mind in the privacy of your own mind those persons who have wronged you and situations in which you feel you have been wronged.

(Pause.)

Leader: Now turn your attention outside yourself to call to mind specific people and situations in which justice is not being done and mercy is called for. You may call to mind conflicts in your church, community, city, country, world. Meditate on the needs of the oppressed for relief.

(Pause.)

[3]But know that the LORD has set apart the faithful for himself;
the LORD hears when I call to him.

Leader: Remember what you know about the compassionate character of God.

(Pause.)

[4]When you are disturbed, do not sin;
ponder it on your beds, and be silent.   *Selah*

Leader: Continue to meditate on the injustice you experience in this world.

(Pause.)

Leader: Now be silent. Turn off your inner chatter. If you can't do this, think of Jesus on the cross, dying for all the sins of the world.

(Pause for an extended period, perhaps even past the point of awkwardness.)

[5]Offer right sacrifices,
and put your trust in the LORD.

Leader: Vow to behave toward others in a more just and compassionate way. Tell God you trust him to take care of your cares as well as those of the world.

> ⁶There are many who say, "O that we might see some good!
> Let the light of your face shine on us, O LORD!"

Leader: Let this call alone be the focus of your attention: that the Lord make his presence known in the inner recesses of your heart and soul.

> ⁷You have put gladness in my heart
> more than when their grain and wine abound.

Leader: If you have experienced in any way a sense of God's dealing with you in the past few minutes, thank him. If you are still troubled, tell him you will trust him with your life anyway.

(Pause.)

Leader: Let's say together the last verse of the psalm:

> ⁸I will both lie down and sleep in peace;
> for you alone, O LORD, make me lie down in safety.

SOME PARTING REMARKS

As you as leader may now realize, people who enter deeply into the experience of prayer may have significant reactions. Be prepared for them to process some of them in the afterglow of your prayer together. You may need to spend time with some of them not only after the prayer but a few days later as well.

A Morning Meditation
Psalm 5

Meditation in the morning: "This is the fittest time for intercourse with God. An hour in the morning is worth two in the evening. While the dew is still on the grass, let the grace of God drop upon the soul." So writes Charles Spurgeon, the great nineteenth-century preacher and expositor of the Psalms. He was clearly a morning person, as we would say today, but also clearly a wise counselor.

It may take some effort to acquire this habit. I am a morning person—not so much as John Wesley, who rose well before dawn to pray, but enough to find morning meditation easier and more productive than evening prayer. To C. Stacey Woods, a person who was formative in the development of my spiritual life, the phrase "morning quiet time" was one word. Prayers in the evening were advisable; those in the morning were demanded. I adopted this rule easily, even though I have not always kept it.

In Psalm 5 we have an ancient Hebrew morning meditation. We will do well to integrate its form and content into our own prayer life.

INITIAL READING OF PSALM 5

Psalm 5

To the leader: for the flutes. A Psalm of David.

[1]Give ear to my words, O LORD;
  give heed to my sighing.
[2]Listen to the sound of my cry,
  my King and my God,
  for to you I pray.
[3]O LORD, in the morning you hear my voice;
  in the morning I plead my case to you and watch.

[4]For you are not a God who delights in wickedness;
  evil will not sojourn with you.
[5]The boastful will not stand before your eyes;
  you hate all evildoers.
[6]You destroy those who speak lies;
  the LORD abhors the bloodthirsty and deceitful.

[7]But I, through the abundance of your steadfast love,
  will enter your house,
 I will bow down toward your holy temple
  in awe of you.
[8]Lead me, O LORD, in your righteousness
  because of my enemies;
  make your way straight before me.

[9]For there is no truth in their mouths;
  their hearts are destruction;
 their throats are open graves;
  they flatter with their tongues.
[10]Make them bear their guilt, O God;
  let them fall by their own counsels;
 because of their many transgressions cast them out,
  for they have rebelled against you.

¹¹But let all who take refuge in you rejoice;
>   let them ever sing for joy.
> Spread your protection over them,
>   so that those who love your name may exult in you.
>¹²For you bless the righteous, O LORD;
>   you cover them with favor as with a shield.

The instructions here for reading each psalm will always be the same: Read and reread this psalm slowly until the words and ideas become embedded in your consciousness. Read it aloud. Read it silently. Read it well. Then you will be ready to study it. That is next. Finally, you will be able to pray it. And that is best.

GETTING AT THE MEANING OF PSALM 5

The troubles that sparked this are mostly a matter of words—words that don't break bones but wound souls. Words indeed can hurt us, but God can bring relief.

Rational Structure

The rational structure of this psalm is not as straightforward as it might appear. As will have become clear in the reading, there is a double ebb and flow.

Invocation

>¹Give ear to my words, O LORD;
>   give heed to my sighing.
>²Listen to the sound of my cry,
>   my King and my God,
>   for to you I pray.

The context of the day

[3]O LORD, in the morning you hear my voice;
>   in the morning I plead my case to you and watch.

God as holy, evildoers as wicked

[4]For you are not a God who delights in wickedness;
>   evil will not sojourn with you.
[5]The boastful will not stand before your eyes;
>   you hate all evildoers.
[6]You destroy those who speak lies;
>   the LORD abhors the bloodthirsty and deceitful.

Confidence before God

[7]But I, through the abundance of your steadfast love,
>   will enter your house,
> I will bow down toward your holy temple
>   in awe of you.
[8]Lead me, O LORD, in your righteousness
>   because of my enemies;
>   make your way straight before me.

The wickedness of the deceitful

[9]For there is no truth in their mouths;
>   their hearts are destruction;
> their throats are open graves;
>   they flatter with their tongues.
[10]Make them bear their guilt, O God;
>   let them fall by their own counsels;
> because of their many transgressions cast them out,

for they have rebelled against you.

Prayer for protection

[11]But let all who take refuge in you rejoice;
>   let them ever sing for joy.
> Spread your protection over them,
>   so that those who love your name may exult in you.

The Lord's blessing

[12]For you bless the righteous, O LORD;
>   you cover them with favor as with a shield.

As in the night thoughts of Psalm 4, the psalmist opens by calling out to God. *Words, sighing, cry, voice, plead:* in the first three verses these are only the first five of many words and phrases that focus on speech. Speech is a central concern of the entire psalm. Here the speech is directed to God, and God is acknowledged as King. The psalmist longs to come into the presence of God, longs for God to hear his lament, his acknowledgment of God's great holiness and power.

It is morning, and as the day stretches out before him, he wakens his attention and turns to God, not because he believes that he can command God to hear him but because he believes God will hear him even if he must wait in watchfulness. To *plead* and to *watch:* this is a frequent rhythm in the psalms and must become so for us. The refrain "how long, O Lord?" comes quickly enough as we wait for God to respond.

I find it striking that what comes next does not focus on the holiness of God but on God who is holy. That is, the psalmist is not abstracting aspects of God's character but attending to God himself. And what he attends to is one of the more awesome and even frightening aspects of

God—his hatred of wickedness, his absolute refusal to abide its presence. The *boastful* and *those who speak lies* must not, who cannot, stand before him, for he hates them and destroys them. Again there is the focus on evil speech—prideful boasts and lying deceit.

There are many "aweful" statements in Psalms. Here is one of them. We are often told by preachers that God hates sin but loves the sinner. But there is no squeezing out of these terrifying lines: *You destroy those who speak lies* and *The boastful will not stand before your eyes.* At this point, the psalmist is not praying that God destroy the wicked. He is only acknowledging that that is what God does without being asked. The psalmist waits till later to pray for God's vengeance, and there his vengefulness is mitigated by his realization that all that must happen is for the logic of the wicked to be worked out.

Who are the wicked? The psalmist may well be talking first of all about his own or Israel's enemies, those from whom he must take refuge (v. 11) and find protection (v. 12). But what about himself? Is he conscious of his own sin? How can he escape God's wrath? And what about me? Can I escape?

It is interesting that the psalmist does not seem to be as troubled by these terrifying words as I am as his reader. I certainly have boasted and am often boastful. Am I damned? True, I do not major in boasting, but I do boast. (I am, I am afraid, boasting when I say this.) True, I do not consciously deceive others, at least not very often. I don't always tell everything I know. Is that deceit? Am I damned?

In any case, the psalmist goes immediately on to contrast himself with the wicked. *I . . . will enter your house, . . . bow down toward your holy temple in awe of you.* Then he prays to be led in the way of the very *righteousness* of God. This, he believes will shield him from his enemies. *Make your way straight before me,* he prays.

How can the psalmist so quickly pass over the possibility of his own wickedness? There is no confession in this psalm. True, Old Testament scholar Peter Craigie speculates that the psalmist may mean to make his acknowledgment of God's hatred of wicked people an implicit confession. But the confession is not explicit. Instead comes a confident assurance that God through his love will let him enter his house of worship and will direct his path.

The ancient psalmist did not know that God was going to solve the problem of sin through the death of his Son. He could only hope for the forgiving love of God revealed on the cross. Today when we read Scripture, we can hear Jesus, the very Son of God, say to the thief who acknowledged his guilt, "Truly I tell you, today you will be with me in Paradise" (Lk 23:43). Still, the psalmist trusts the God who is righteous to also be one who protects and saves. This I too, and you, dear reader, can also do, with even more reason.

Then comes a second wave of recrimination. The wicked rise again in the consciousness of the psalmist, and he lays bare their verbal sins— *no truth in their mouths, their throats are open graves, they flatter with their tongues.* He calls for God to let the causal nexus, the system of natural causes, take its toll: *let them fall by their own counsels.* The only sin not directly associated with speech is that *their hearts are destruction,* and the punishment is being *cast out* for their rebellion. The sins of the tongue should be a main focus when we pray this prayer. In fact, since so much of our day is taken up with discourse, it should be a frequent focus of all our morning prayers.

The psalmist ends his psalm with a call to *rejoice* and *sing* (another speech word), a prayer for God to protect all his righteous children, those who love his name, and an acknowledgment of God's blessing on those he favors with protection.

Emotional Structure

This is a short psalm; the emotions are few but intense.

- forthright intense and expectant plea to be heard (vv. 1-2)
- relaxed tension as the psalmist waits and watches (v. 3)
- intense, confident but awe-full reliance on a righteous God (vv. 4-6)
- relaxed tension as the psalmist finds himself nearing the presence of God (v. 7)
- return to greater tension as he requests protection and guidance (v. 8)
- rising anger and vengefulness against the wicked (vv. 9-10)
- relaxed tension and a move to joyful worship (v. 11)
- peaceful, relaxed resolution of the emotions (v. 12)

When we pray the psalm, we may find our own emotions slowly come to parallel his.

PRAYING PSALM 5

Read through the entire psalm again. Then, with eyes open, read and pray section by section. The instructions assume that this will be a morning prayer, but the instructions can easily be adapted to fit other situations. Especially appropriate will be those times when one is oppressed by false accusations.

¹Give ear to my words, O LORD;
> give heed to my sighing.
²Listen to the sound of my cry,
> my King and my God,
> for to you I pray.
³O LORD, in the morning you hear my voice;
> in the morning I plead my case to you and watch.

Respond: *Lord, I come to you this morning refreshed from my night of rest. Now as I face the day, I sigh, for I do not know all the joys and troubles I will face. But I know they will be there. Here are the concerns most on my mind.* Mention in turn the situations and problems you believe you will face. Lay each of them before God. After each one, pause for a time. Wait silently, open to hear the voice of God. He may bring to mind things that will help. If, as you raise the issues before God, you find anxiety rising, stop. Go back to verses 1-3 and read them again. This time pause to consider what it means for God to be King. Then continue as a supplicant to present your concerns before the King. After your last issue, continue to pray the psalm.

> [4]For you are not a God who delights in wickedness;
>> evil will not sojourn with you.
> [5]The boastful will not stand before your eyes;
>> you hate all evildoers.
> [6]You destroy those who speak lies;
>> the LORD abhors the bloodthirsty and deceitful.

Respond: *Lord, you are most righteous. You do not delight in the wickedness we face every day. But I know that the proud and haughty have no standing with you. You will not forever let evil men and women work their ways. They will be destroyed. Please strengthen my resolve to do good—to speak no lies, to practice no deceit, to live before my friends and my enemies as one made in your image and redeemed by your Son.*

But let me reflect as well. I realize my own spiritual and moral weakness. Where I am sinful, show me my guilt and forgive my transgressions. (Here you may list those you are aware of.) *Cleanse me of my hidden faults. Forgive me for my sins.*

> [7]But I, through the abundance of your steadfast love,
>> will enter your house,
> I will bow down toward your holy temple
>> in awe of you.

Respond: *Lord, in the quietness of this place where I now am, let me enter your presence. I bow in awe before you.* In silence spend some minutes contemplating the great holiness and power of God. Then continue to pray the psalm.

> [8]Lead me, O LORD, in your righteousness
> > because of my enemies;
> > make your way straight before me.

Respond: *Indeed, Lord, as I face the troubles of the day, lead me to act as you would act, to imitate your righteousness in my actions. You have forgiven me. Let me act as one forgiven—and purified as well. Guide me, O thou great Jehovah! Make the crooked path before me straight.* Here you might ask for specific guidance on those decisions you know you must make today or very soon.

> [9]For there is no truth in their mouths;
> > their hearts are destruction;
> > their throats are open graves;
> > they flatter with their tongues.
> [10]Make them bear their guilt, O God;
> > let them fall by their own counsels;
> > because of their many transgressions cast them out,
> > for they have rebelled against you.

Respond: Contemplate the picture drawn in verse 9 of mouth, heart, throat and tongue. *I cannot get them out of my mind, Lord—those around me who lie, who breathe out obnoxious odors of deceit and villainy. And those in our country and abroad who cheat and oppress the poor and the weak. Let them becomes victims of their own fraud and ill-counsel. I will not take vengeance on them but leave in your hands the fate of those who rebel against you and against your good will.*

> [11]But let all who take refuge in you rejoice;

let them ever sing for joy.
Spread your protection over them,
    so that those who love your name may exult in you.

Respond: *Now I take refuge in you. I take leave of my efforts to run my own life and to save myself with bumbling attempts at good deeds. I take refuge in you. May all your children take refuge in you. Then may they sing for joy.* You might sing a praise song at this point.

[12]For you bless the righteous, O LORD;
    you cover them with favor as with a shield.

Respond: *O Lord, you are the righteous Lord. And you bless the righteous. You protect them as with a shield. As I end this prayer, I continue to live in its spirit. In my going and coming I will seek to remain in the spirit of waiting and watching. Amen.*

SOME FURTHER REFLECTIONS

This psalm, like Psalm 4, could well be prayed repeatedly over an extended period of time—a week or two every once in a while. It can set the day on the right track. But then so can many psalms. The point is to so enter into its spirit that it becomes a pattern for life.

Small Group Study of Psalm 5

The following comments are directed to the leader.

Introduction

This psalm was used in ancient Hebrew public worship and is easily applicable to group use today.

Group Instruction and Questions

1. Have one person read Psalm 5 in its entirety at an ordinary pace.

2. Have another person read it very slowly, with a pause after each verse.

3. A third reading would be appropriate—but not if it looks as if people in the group are getting restless.

4. Why is the morning an appropriate time for this prayer?

5. What does the psalmist want God to do immediately (vv. 1-3)?

6. What troubles the psalmist (vv. 4-6, 9-10)?

   Why do you think he speaks of this trouble in two different sets of verses?

7. What kind of wickedness gets the most attention? (When this has been answered, have someone list the phrases that have to do with sins of the tongue.)

   Why do you think the psalmist might have been so concerned with these sorts of sin? (This is a speculative question but should elicit such answers as these: His enemies have been slandering him; he has been a victim of deceit; he believes that God has been blasphemed by what has been said.)

8. Give some modern examples of sins of the tongue. Have some of them caused the sinner to suffer unhappy consequences?

9. How does the psalmist react to the sins of the tongue?

   How do you react to this list of sins: with a sense of guilt or with the psalmist's sense of innocence?

   In either case, what should you do?

10. How do you feel about calling on God for vengeance against the wicked?

   What makes you feel that way? (Tell the group that such cries for vengeance are frequent in the psalms and they often rightfully disturb us. Tell them, too, that they will be considered in some depth when you meditate on Psalm 137 in chapter eight.)

11. What causes the psalmist to rejoice (vv. 11-12)? How is this justified by what has come before in the psalm?

   When you as leader believe the group is ready to make Psalm 5 its corporate prayer, proceed as directed.

Directed Prayer

The following script may help the group to pray the psalm.

Leader: Let us pray through Psalm 5. Let's say the first two verses together:

> [1]Give ear to my words, O LORD;
> > give heed to my sighing.
> [2]Listen to the sound of my cry,
> > my King and my God,
> > for to you I pray.

Leader: Reflect on what it means to enter the presence of the King of creation and present your prayers.

(Pause.)

> ³O LORD, in the morning you hear my voice;
>> in the morning I plead my case to you and watch.

Leader: Pause now. Be quiet before the Lord.

> (Pause. Let the group be silent for a couple of minutes.)

> ⁴For you are not a God who delights in wickedness;
>> evil will not sojourn with you.
> ⁵The boastful will not stand before your eyes;
>> you hate all evildoers.
> ⁶You destroy those who speak lies;
>> the LORD abhors the bloodthirsty and deceitful.

Leader: Consider the plight of the wicked—the boastful, the evildoers, the bloodthirsty, the deceitful.

(Pause.)

Leader: Now consider your place before the King. Given that the wicked cannot stand there, can you stand? Do you need to confess any sin? Do that silently now. Ask God's forgiveness. Accept his acceptance. Realize this: "There is therefore now no condemnation for those who are in Christ Jesus. For the law of the Spirit of life in Christ Jesus has set you free from the law of sin and of death" (Rom 8:1-2). Wait for the awesome wonder of this to sink deep into your consciousness.

(Pause.)

> ⁷But I, through the abundance of your steadfast love,
>> will enter your house,

I will bow down toward your holy temple
    in awe of you.

Leader: Glory in the wonder of God's presence.
    (Pause.)

[8]Lead me, O LORD, in your righteousness
    because of my enemies;
    make your way straight before me.

Leader: Pray silently now for guidance as you look forward to decisions you must soon make or anything that seems to obscure or block God's path for you. If you are troubled by people who seem bent on hurting you or blocking your goals or God's goals, bring them before the Lord and leave them. Rely on God, and determine to let him make your path straight before you.

(Pause.)

Leader: Now think again about the evil, especially of sins of the tongue.

[9]For there is no truth in their mouths;
    their hearts are destruction;
  their throats are open graves;
    they flatter with their tongues.

Leader: Paint a picture in your mind's eye of the scene just described—the truthless mouth, the destructive heart, the graveyard of open throats, the flattering tongue. Smell the ugly stench of the wicked liars.

[10]Make them bear their guilt, O God;
    let them fall by their own counsels;
  because of their many transgressions cast them out,
    for they have rebelled against you.

Leader: Turn over to God the fate of evildoers. Turn back from thoughts of personal vengeance against either God's enemies or your own. Let justice roll down from God alone.

> [11]But let all who take refuge in you rejoice;
>   let them ever sing for joy.

Leader: Look forward in hope to God's solution to your problems, to his removal of your enemies so that they cannot block God's righteous path for you. We have told God that we were going to plead our case before him (v. 3) and then *watch*. Let us do so by pausing in silence.

(Pause. This pause may be longer than most. Use your judgment as to how long, but let it be more than three minutes. Then return to pray the remainder of the psalm.)

> Spread your protection over them,
>   so that those who love your name may exult in you.
> [12]For you bless the righteous, O LORD;
>   you cover them with favor as with a shield.

Leader: Thank God for his great favor to us. (Sing together a hymn or praise song.)

SOME PARTING REMARKS

You may wish to encourage group members to pray this psalm on their own for the next few mornings, to let its pattern sink into their subconscious and serve as a guide to future prayer.

As with Psalm 4, be prepared to listen to those who want to share with you or the group some of what they have just experienced.

Thirsting for God
Psalms 42—43

The opening lines of Psalm 42 are among the most poignant lines in all of poetry:

> As the deer pants for streams of water,
>> so my soul pants for you, O God.

These lines arrest our attention. Then, verse by verse, the psalm holds our attention as it both reveals the soul of the psalmist and probes our own souls. We should come away from praying this psalm with a deeper grasp of our own self and a stronger sense of our need for the presence of God.

Each time I read Psalms 42—43, the impact of that reading is added to the impact of former readings. Phrase after phrase reminds me of what I have read before but had receded to the dimly lit warehouse of my memory. But as you are praying through the psalms, you are seeing this for yourself.

Two words of warning. First, Psalms 42—43 are more complex in both structure and meaning than the previous psalms. Be prepared to spend more time in reading before beginning to pray. Second, Psalms 42—43 are especially relevant to those who are disappointed or depressed. The guided prayer assumes that this issue will be relevant to many, though perhaps not all, readers.

INITIAL READING OF PSALM 42

From even a cursory examination of the texts, it seems obvious that Psalms 42 and 43 are really one psalm. And scholars largely agree. Both the formal structure and the intellectual content confirm this judgment. So we will read them as a unit.

Psalm 42 (NIV)

For the director of music. A *maskil* of the Sons of Korah.

> [1]As the deer pants for streams of water,
>> so my soul pants for you, O God.
> [2]My soul thirsts for God, for the living God.
>> When can I go and meet with God?
> [3]My tears have been my food
>> day and night,
> while men say to me all day long,
>> "Where is your God?"
> [4]These things I remember
>> as I pour out my soul:
> how I used to go with the multitude,
>> leading the procession to the house of God,
> with shouts of joy and thanksgiving
>> among the festive throng.
>
> [5]Why are you downcast, O my soul?
>> Why so disturbed within me?
> Put your hope in God,

for I will yet praise him,
   my Savior and [6]my God.

My soul is downcast within me;
      therefore I will remember you
from the land of the Jordan,
      the heights of Hermon—from Mount Mizar.
[7]Deep calls to deep
      in the roar of your waterfalls;
all your waves and breakers
      have swept over me.

[8]By day the LORD directs his love,
      at night his song is with me—
      a prayer to the God of my life.

[9]I say to God my Rock,
      "Why have you forgotten me?
Why must I go about mourning,
      oppressed by the enemy?"
[10]My bones suffer mortal agony
      as my foes taunt me,
saying to me all day long,
      "Where is your God?"

[11]Why are you downcast, O my soul?
      Why so disturbed within me?
Put your hope in God,
      for I will yet praise him,
      my Savior and my God.

Psalm 43

[1]Vindicate me, O God,
>   and plead my cause against an ungodly nation;
> rescue me from deceitful and wicked men.
[2]You are God my stronghold.
>   Why have you rejected me?
> Why must I go about mourning,
>   oppressed by the enemy?
[3]Send forth your light and your truth,
>   let them guide me;
> let them bring me to your holy mountain,
>   to the place where you dwell.
[4]Then will I go to the altar of God,
>   to God, my joy and my delight.
> I will praise you with the harp,
>   O God, my God.

[5]Why are you downcast, O my soul?
>   Why so disturbed within me?
> Put your hope in God,
>   for I will yet praise him,
>   my Savior and my God.

When you read this just now, did you read it aloud? If not, do so now. Then read it silently several more times. Observe what verse(s), ideas or images seem to stand out most.

INITIAL IMPRESSIONS

With each reading, what attracts my attention at one time may not at all be what attracts me at another. The opening lines, however, always stand out:

> [1]As the deer pants for streams of water,
>> so my soul pants for you, O God.
> [2]My soul thirsts for God, for the living God.
>> When can I go and meet with God?

Each time I read this, there is at once a recognition that I too long for, thirst for, the living God; and then immediately follows the recognition that if I really did long for the living God as a deer pants for streams of water, God would be present to my consciousness far more than he is. So the psalm sets me up to recognize a paradox that I live with whenever I turn my attention toward it:

> I long for the presence of God.
> I do not long for the presence of God.

At times—when I am deliberately disobeying (and I do that; don't you?)—I don't want God to be present at all. The question *When can I go and meet with God?* is not the one in my heart, for I know the answer. The answer is "Anytime!" The answer is "Now."

The more I read the psalm, the more I am conscious of this schism in my soul. And the more I need to continue to read and absorb the psalm, for there is a division in the psyche of the psalmist too. Three times the psalmist asks himself the same question. Three times he answers the same way.

> [5]Why are you downcast, O my soul?
>> Why so disturbed within me?
> Put your hope in God,
>> for I will yet praise him,
>> my Savior and [6]my God.

Of course, these lines are a refrain. Poems sometimes have refrains. They have a formal function in the poem. Why make any more of them than that? In great poetry, the content of a refrain and the necessity of its repetition yield a significance of sense. So it does here.

The psalmist reveals that he himself is divided. One aspect of himself (unnamed) addresses another aspect of himself (his soul). Bemused and troubled about his depression, he asks his soul to put its hope in God, and he vows to praise God as *my Savior and my God.* Thus the downcast soul seeks solace in praising his God as his Savior. The psalmist speaks the lines of this refrain without hesitation and with authority. He knows this is the right path to take, and so do I, both from the implicit authority I accord the Scriptures and from the experience of having followed the psalmist's lead before.

As I reflect on the many times I have read and reread Psalm 42, my impression is that the opening lines and the refrain are its core—that if we would only absorb and live by these words, our lives and the lives of many others would benefit. But, of course, the psalm has much more to offer, and more than these lines stand out.

MISUNDERSTANDING THE DEEP

This psalm is one of my favorites. I enjoy contemplating philosophic issues. Once when I was dealing with the relationship between the surface of life (the impressions made on us through our five senses) and the depths of Being itself (the "isness" of what is), verse 7 jumped off the page for me:

> ⁷Deep calls to deep
> > in the roar of your waterfalls;
> > all your waves and breakers
> > > have swept over me.

Deep calls to deep, I read. What *deep?* In the metaphor of the psalm the deep, I thought, is the ocean deep and God himself beneath the ocean deep. This deep calls to other depths, my depths. Or, in less metaphoric terms, the foundations of reality (ocean depths), created by and present to God himself, call to the foundations of my being (my depths), likewise created by God. Moreover, in the foundation of my being (my depths) is found the unity of my soul and the unnamed part of me that speaks to my soul. In the language of verse 7, therefore, I felt my divided self both unify and be brought into communion with God and his created order. I saw myself grounded (to shift the metaphor) in God. God is there in the depths of the created order, I thought, and God is there in the depths of my own being.

So fully is God there that his waterfalls roar and his waves swamp me with their presence. As I contemplated this image, I was reminded of a dream a few nights before. I was in a cottage near a seashore and a twenty-foot sea surge swept over the cottage. Of course, I woke up before I was drowned. But in Psalm 42 I took the overwhelming cataract as an image of the presence of God. It was God who had swamped the psalmist. At rare times the presence of God swamps me as well. Sometimes in silence and solitude my attention is given to the depths that sustain me, and then the deep itself—the reality of God—surges through me. Unfortunately, this impressionistic reading is significantly in error.

UNDERSTANDING THE DEEP

When I consulted the work of biblical scholars, I learned that I had misunderstood *Deep calls to deep* (v. 7). Old Testament scholar Peter Craigie writes that when in verses 6-7 the psalmist tries to recall the times he has been close to God (those mountaintop experiences we all have on occasion), all he can recall is an overwhelming experience of chaos. "He had

longed for the waters of refreshment, but somehow in the effort to remember God, he had unleashed the primeval waters of chaos, which seem
to depict so powerfully his terrible situation."

Derek Kidner agrees. *Deep*, he says, is the same word used in Genesis 1:2,
where "darkness was over the surface of the deep, and the Spirit of God
was hovering over the waters" (NIV), and it thus suggests chaos or the unformed creation. Kidner writes: "Here is the picture of all that is overwhelming: his footing gone, and wave after wave submerging him. This is
the language that Jonah takes up in the depths (*cf.* 7b with Jon. 2:3)."

Charles Spurgeon, in one of his frequent displays of purple prose, as-
sociates the *deep* with the terrors of the sea and the satanic forces symbol-
ized by it. What I have seen as giving the psalmist hope as the depths of
God call to the depths of the psalmist, Spurgeon sees as terrifying:

> Billow followed billow, one sea echoed the roaring of another;
> bodily pain aroused mental fear, Satanic suggestions chimed in with
> inward anguish: his soul seemed drowned as in a universal deluge of
> trouble, over whose waves the providence of the Lord moved as a
> watery pillar, in dreadful majesty inspiring the utmost terror. As for
> the afflicted one he was like a lonely bark around which the fury of
> a storm is bursting, or a mariner floating on a mast, almost every
> moment submerged.

Let preachers take note. It is hard to improve on the simplicity of great
poetry. The spare eloquence of *Deep calls to deep* is a picture that is worth a
thousand elaborations.

Finally, the discussion of *deep* in *The Dictionary of Biblical Imagery* is without qualification: "From the beginning of Scripture to the end, references
to 'the deep' and 'the depths' are images of terror with associations of
danger, chaos, malevolent evil and death. 'The deep' is a major negative

archetype in the biblical imagination—a place or state of mind or soul
that one would wish to avoid but that no one can completely avoid."

The negative quality of *deep*, it would seem, must replace my own impressionistic reading.

MORE INITIAL IMPRESSIONS

During my various readings of this psalm, other lines come to the surface:

> ³My tears have been my food
>   day and night,
>   while men say to me all day long,
>   "Where is your God?"

But these lines are different. The reason they surface is not that they
are relevant but that they are—at least for some time—not what I experience at all. They do not fit my present life. What am I to make of them?
Even the lines that follow do not summon up memories:

> ⁴These things I remember
>   as I pour out my soul:
>   how I used to go with the multitude,
>   leading the procession to the house of God,
>   with shouts of joy and thanksgiving
>   among the festive throng.

The psalmist is recalling joyous ritual processions in which he participated. He is contrasting past joy with present despair. But I am not in
despair, nor can I think of any rituals that have inspired in me the joy of
the psalmist. I am not very emotional, or so I think; I do not suffer from
low lows nor celebrate with high highs. So this part of the psalm remains
to be appreciated from a distance. I know others who do have such expe-

riences. So I take some vicarious, distanced, even perhaps aesthetic pleasure in the language and the images that are evoked. My reading becomes a window on the reality of others, a reality I learn to appreciate as I pray with them the words of these verses.

The same experience faces me in these more tense verses:

> [9]I say to God my Rock,
>> "Why have you forgotten me?
>> Why must I go about mourning,
>>> oppressed by the enemy?"
> [10]My bones suffer mortal agony
>> as my foes taunt me,
>> saying to me all day long,
>>> "Where is your God?"

Here, however, I have come to see the personal relevance of these lines in two ways. First, they are always apt in a general way. Our real enemy is not the material forces that threaten us with physical slavery, imprisonment and death. In the final analysis, our enemy is Satan himself, who "prowls around like a roaring lion looking for someone to devour" (1 Pet 5:8 NIV). His oppression is always a possibility and often a reality; temptation is our constant companion. When we are beset by strong but wrong desires, it is always tempting to ask, "Where are you, God? Why do you not transform me so that my desires are your desires?"

Second, there are many Christians and others too who are physically oppressed. Stories in the papers and on television are legion. Closer to me are my friends who are in these situations, notably Africa—Mozambique, Uganda, Nigeria, Kenya. I read letters from them, and they are often in my prayers. Now, as I reflect on these verses, they come to mind again. My friends' experience is literally that of the psalmist. And I ask with them, not "Where is their God?" but "Where is my God?" These verses raise for me the most difficult of biblical, theological, philosophical conundrums: Why doesn't a God who is infinitely good and infinitely powerful either prevent the tragic tsunamis and floods, the mass killings, the ravages of disease or redress such wrongs in a much more obvious fashion? The problem of evil is both age-old and profound. And it gets the same answer now as it did long ago: Soul, put your hope in God.

In what we know as Psalm 43, the issue is made even clearer:

> ¹Vindicate me, O God,
>
>> and plead my cause against an ungodly nation;
>> rescue me from deceitful and wicked men.
>
> ²You are God my stronghold.
>
>> Why have you rejected me?
>
> Why must I go about mourning,
>
>> oppressed by the enemy?

I can and do pray this in the name of my oppressed brothers and sisters, those I know personally and those I know only from news stories and pictures. In intense reading, in reading and rereading, in praying the psalm, there comes a sense of communion. I do not say unity, for that is to claim too much for physically painless empathy to claim; it would trivialize the deep and agonized suffering of flesh-and-blood men, women and children. Still, I can readily pray these lines with the psalmist:

> ³Send forth your light and your truth,
>
>> let them guide me;
>
> let them bring me to your holy mountain,
>
>> to the place where you dwell.
>
> ⁴Then will I go to the altar of God,

to God, my joy and my delight.
I will praise you with the harp,
O God, my God.

Surely this is a prayer God wants us all to pray. That we have to wait for deliverance from evil and its power again becomes a problem. So I am returned to contemplating the misery of others and resurrecting the specter of the downcast soul.

[5]Why are you downcast, O my soul?
Why so disturbed within me?

Yet now I see more fully the aptness of the psalmist's address to his soul:

Put your hope in God,
for I will yet praise him,
my Savior and my God.

We have looked at Psalms 42—43 first from the standpoint of my own deep impressions after reading and rereading it. But we need to look further. We need to see the psalm as a whole, and we need to check my impressions with more careful study. To see the psalm as a whole, we need to do at least two things: (1) know what each of the parts means and (2) know its overall structure, the flow of its "argument." First we will deal with the easier of the two—knowing what the parts mean.

CLARIFYING THE DETAILS

In Psalm 42—43 there are three geographical allusions: Jordan, Hermon and Mount Mizar.

Jordan is, of course, the main river in Israel, and so the land of Jordan must be somewhere in its proximity. Kidner identifies the waterfall of

42:7 with the Jordan River near its source on Mount Hermon, which is in the north of Israel. *Mount Mizar* ("smallness"), he says, "was evidently part of a range which Hermon dominated, but it is so far unidentified."

Does this information add anything to our reading? Perhaps. Kidner, for example, suggests that these psalms are the "lament of a temple singer exiled in the north near the rising Jordan, who longs to be back at God's house, and turns his longing into resolute faith and hope in God Himself." There is really no telling evidence to confirm the speculation, but it does suggest what was surely the case—that the psalm reflects the nature of discouragement and despair. Such psychological and spiritual realism must have had its roots in the experience of the psalmist. If he was not exiled in the north, it was as if he were. Such an outer geographical setting is a fitting counterpart to the inner psychological condition.

But more important than the physical streams of water—the River Jordan and the ocean deeps—is what they symbolize. This is in the final analysis not a psalm about a person who would like to attend his home church but has been sent on a long journey where there are no churches. It is a psalm about that profound spiritual dryness that comes at all kinds of times in our life, often not prompted by anything we can identify as its cause. We are home, but we feel as if we were away. We are in church, but God is no more present to us than when we were at the movies the night before. So the physical details serve not as the point of the psalm but the symbolic structure, the grammar, of our experience.

RESPITE FROM DESPAIR OR A PRAYER IN HOPE

Scholars make few comments about verse 8, apparently not seeing any puzzle about its place in the psalm. But I have not found it easy to determine whether it describes a break in the psalmist's mood of despair or a picture of what he is praying for.

[8]By day the LORD directs his love,
    at night his song is with me—
    a prayer to the God of my life.

The first two lines come immediately after the psalmist's experience of the waters of chaos. Has God suddenly come to him, satisfying his longing for the water brooks of God's presence? That seems possible. But then comes a line restating his despair. Is it not more likely that the vision of God's presence is itself the prayer? Prayer that rests on hope: this seems to me to be the only relief found within the psalm itself.

DISCERNING THE STRUCTURE

Since the thrice-repeated refrains are unmistakable, we don't need a learned scholar to show us the formal structure. Still, Craigie states it with utmost simplicity:

1. 42:2-6	(a) Lament (vv 2-5)
	(b) *Refrain* (v 6)
2. 42:7-12	(a) Lament (vv 7-11)
	(b) *Refrain* (v 12)
3. 43:1-5	(a) Lament (vv 1-4)
	(b) *Refrain* (v 5)

What is not so clear in Psalms 42—43, however, is the *rational structure*, that is, the specific flow of ideas and the reason for that flow. Elaborating on Craigie's formal structure, we can discern the following:

I.   First statement of the problem: Unquenched thirst for God

[1]As the deer pants for streams of water,
    so my soul pants for you, O God.
[2]My soul thirsts for God, for the living God.

When can I go and meet with God?

Elaboration of the problem

[3]My tears have been my food
>day and night,
while men say to me all day long,
>"Where is your God?"

Memory of good times

[4]These things I remember
>as I pour out my soul:
how I used to go with the multitude,
>leading the procession to the house of God,
with shouts of joy and thanksgiving
>among the festive throng.

Refrain I: Despair and hope for relief

[5]Why are you downcast, O my soul?
>Why so disturbed within me?
Put your hope in God,
>for I will yet praise him,
>my Savior and [6]my God.

II. Second statement of the problem: Despair

My soul is downcast within me;
>therefore I will remember you
from the land of the Jordan,
>the heights of Hermon—from Mount Mizar.

Elaboration of the problem: Overwhelming despair

[7]Deep calls to deep
>in the roar of your waterfalls;

all your waves and breakers
    have swept over me.

A prayer from the depths
[8]By day the LORD directs his love,
    at night his song is with me—
    a prayer to the God of my life.
[9]I say to God my Rock,
    "Why have you forgotten me?
    Why must I go about mourning,
    oppressed by the enemy?"

Problem elaborated
[10]My bones suffer mortal agony
    as my foes taunt me,
saying to me all day long,
    "Where is your God?"

Refrain 2: Despair and hope for relief
[11]Why are you downcast, O my soul?
    Why so disturbed within me?
Put your hope in God,
    for I will yet praise him,
    my Savior and my God.

III. Prayer for deliverance from the wicked world
[1]Vindicate me, O God,
    and plead my cause against an ungodly nation;
    rescue me from deceitful and wicked men.
[2]You are God my stronghold.

Why have you rejected me?
Why must I go about mourning,
   oppressed by the enemy?

Prayer for guidance to the presence of God

³Send forth your light and your truth,
   let them guide me;
let them bring me to your holy mountain,
   to the place where you dwell.

Vision of worship when his prayer is answered

⁴Then will I go to the altar of God,
   to God, my joy and my delight.
I will praise you with the harp,
   O God, my God.

Refrain 3: Despair and hope of relief

⁵Why are you downcast, O my soul?
   Why so disturbed within me?
Put your hope in God,
   for I will yet praise him,
   my Savior and my God.

This bare outline of the psalm is rough and inexact. Still, it helps us
see that three times the psalmist presents his case before God, each time
in a different way, but each time with the same result. The life of the
psalm, however, is not in the outline but in the verse-by-verse revelation
of the depths of the psalmist's despair and his tenacious hope that one
day relief and resolution will come.

PRAYING PSALMS 42—43

Read through both psalms again. Then read and pray section by section. This directed prayer assumes a reader sympathetic to the theme of discouragement and despair.

> ¹As the deer pants for streams of water,
>> so my soul pants for you, O God.
> ²My soul thirsts for God, for the living God.
>> When can I go and meet with God?

Respond: *Lord, I yearn to be in your presence. Will you come now? Is there another time? When can I meet you?*

> ³My tears have been my food
>> day and night,
> while men say to me all day long,
>> "Where is your God?"

Respond: *I hear the psalmist in his agony. I too have felt this way in those frequent dry periods when you seem so far away.* Make the psalm personal here. Tell God where you believe you stand with him now. Verbalize how you feel as you seek his presence.

> ⁴These things I remember
>> as I pour out my soul:
> how I used to go with the multitude,
>> leading the procession to the house of God,
> with shouts of joy and thanksgiving
>> among the festive throng.

Respond: *Lord, I have had some very good times with you.* Reflect on the times when you have felt God's presence, when you have joyfully participated in

worship, when you have communed with God in prayer and meditation.
Tell him how much you have appreciated these special times.

> [5]Why are you downcast, O my soul?
>> Why so disturbed within me?
> Put your hope in God,
>> for I will yet praise him,
>> my Savior and [6]my God.

Respond: *Lord, this is precisely how I feel. My soul is downcast. I don't know why.*
But longingly I put my hope in you, for you are my Savior and my God.

This refrain will occur three times. Each time you may have a different
reaction. As you pray, God may respond with a distinct sense of his affirming presence. In that case, thank him and pray for others.

> My soul is downcast within me;
>> therefore I will remember you
> from the land of the Jordan,
>> the heights of Hermon—from Mount Mizar.

Respond: *Lord, I do recall some very special times with you.* Pause to reflect and
then identify those times of peak experience.

> [7]Deep calls to deep
>> in the roar of your waterfalls;
> all your waves and breakers
>> have swept over me.

Respond: If when you recall the good times God again becomes real, thank
him. If you continue to be overwhelmed by your present despair, then return to prayer: *Lord, I am overwhelmed by sorrow, by despair, by loneliness. I feel I have*
no one to help me. My friends are gone. My life is empty. Elaborate in your own words.

⁸By day the LORD directs his love,
    at night his song is with me—
    a prayer to the God of my life.

Respond: *Lord, this is my prayer for a life filled with your love.*
    Pause to contemplate the joy in God's presence that you are yearning for.

⁹I say to God my Rock,
        "Why have you forgotten me?
    Why must I go about mourning,
        oppressed by the enemy?"
¹⁰My bones suffer mortal agony
        as my foes taunt me,
    saying to me all day long,
        "Where is your God?"

Respond: *Lord, I don't know why I feel so far from you. But I do know that I am being harassed by people who do not believe in you.*

¹¹Why are you downcast, O my soul?
        Why so disturbed within me?
    Put your hope in God,
        for I will yet praise him,
        my Savior and my God.

Respond: *Lord, again I place my despair in your hands. Establish my hope. Keep me steady. Someday I will indeed yet praise you in freedom and joy. You are my hope.*

¹Vindicate me, O God,
        and plead my cause against an ungodly nation;
        rescue me from deceitful and wicked men.
²You are God my stronghold.

Why have you rejected me?
Why must I go about mourning,
oppressed by the enemy?

Respond: *Lord, I have been working your will, living for you, in a tough and thankless world.* Bring before the Lord those people and forces that are hindering your kingdom living. *Lord, I languish before you, lonely and abandoned.*

[3]Send forth your light and your truth,
let them guide me;
let them bring me to your holy mountain,
to the place where you dwell.

Respond: *I seek, Lord, your guidance. What am I to do to come into your presence? I seek your light and your truth in Scripture. Bring its meaning into the light. Lift me up to you.*
(Pause.)

[4]Then will I go to the altar of God,
to God, my joy and my delight.
I will praise you with the harp,
O God, my God.

(Pause.)

[5]Why are you downcast, O my soul?
Why so disturbed within me?
Put your hope in God,
for I will yet praise him,
my Savior and my God.

Respond: On this the third occasion of this refrain, put your prayer emphasis on the final three lines. *Lord, I put my hope in you. I praise you, my Savior and my God.*

SOME INSIGHTS ON PRAYER

What can we learn about prayer from this psalm? At least three very important things.

First, we should pray with the full arsenal of our emotions open to God. The psalmist begins with a plaintive cry; we may do so too. It is okay to bare our emotions before God. The psalmist even does so in public, not to seek pity from his community but in candor.

Second, we should continue praying, not making a one-time request but elaborating on our pleas, casting them in different ways, working out our frustrations by verbalizing our complaints—and doing so not to the public but to God who alone can answer rightly. The ancient psalmist is our model for extended, agonized petition. Even when our prayers are not being answered as we wish, we should keep on praying.

Third, we should continue living in hope, expecting one day to receive an answer, understand it and praise our Savior and our God. The last two lines of the refrain encourage us to keep on hoping.

Small Group Study of Psalms 42—43

The following comments are directed to the leader.

Introduction

This psalm is especially relevant for those participants who are discouraged. Most groups will include members who are struggling with spiritual dryness, perhaps despair. The study is directed toward them. Those who are not facing such trouble should still be able to contribute to the study and sympathize with the prayers of those who are.

Group Instruction and Questions

1. Have one person read Psalms 42—43 in their entirety at an ordinary pace.

2. Why are these two psalms considered as one?

3. Have another person read them very slowly, with a pause after each verse.

4. Continue with a third reading.

5. Explain that the focus of the study will be on those who find the psalm to be addressing aspects of their life today. Ask the rest to participate with them sympathetically.

6. What yearning is the psalmist concerned with?

   Are any of you willing to say something about your own present or past loss of the sense of God's presence? (Do not press this question. Move on quickly if no one speaks.)

7. What verse is repeated three times (42:5, 11 and 43:5)?

   What does this show about the psalmist's progress in getting a sense of God's presence?

8. Explain the flow of ideas and emotions in the psalm. (If the group contains some mature readers, you may have them all try to outline the emotional and rational flow of the psalm. If this exercise is too difficult or time consuming, use the outline on pp. 97-99. The idea is to understand the shifts in the psalmist's own experience of discouragement and hope.)

9. How does the psalmist's memory of his own peak experience (vv. 4, 6) help him? (This should raise good discussion. Memory is given a significant place in the Hebrew mindset. The prophets often called on the Israelites to remember how God had helped their nation in the past. The exodus from Egypt, for example, was usually not far from the Hebrew mind.)

10. Explain *Deep calls to deep*. (You may need to explain this image to the group; see pp. 89-92.) How is this image an apt picture of despair?

11. The psalmist states his problem three times (42:1, 6 and 43:1). His despair seems to be caused by more than one thing. Identify them.

   Which ones seem most relevant to you today?

12. How are the psalmist's experience and his prayer helpful to you today? (Tell the group that after the prayer you will ask the same question.)

DIRECTED PRAYER

Leader: Let us pray through Psalms 42—43, beginning by saying the first two verses together:

> [1]As the deer pants for streams of water,
>   so my soul pants for you, O God.
> [2]My soul thirsts for God, for the living God.

When can I go and meet with God?

Leader: Make these two verses your prayer by saying them silently to God.
(Pause.)

> [3]My tears have been my food
>   day and night,
> while men say to me all day long,
>   "Where is your God?"

Leader: Imagine the despairing psalmist at prayer, saying these words. If they are yours as well, make them yours. Make the psalm personal. Tell God where you believe you stand with him now. Verbalize silently how you feel now as you seek his presence.

(Pause.)

> [4]These things I remember
>   as I pour out my soul:
> how I used to go with the multitude,
>   leading the procession to the house of God,
> with shouts of joy and thanksgiving
>   among the festive throng.

Leader: Reflect on the times when you have felt God's presence, when you have joyfully participated in worship, when you have communed with God in prayer and meditation. Tell him how much you have appreciated these special times.

(Pause.)

> [5]Why are you downcast, O my soul?
>   Why so disturbed within me?
> Put your hope in God,

for I will yet praise him,
  my Savior and [6]my God.

Leader: Meditate silently on this verse.

(Pause.)

This refrain will occur three times. Each time you may have a different reaction. As you pray, God may respond with a distinct sense of his affirming presence. In that case, thank him and pray for others.

My soul is downcast within me;
    therefore I will remember you
from the land of the Jordan,
    the heights of Hermon—from Mount Mizar.
[7]Deep calls to deep
    in the roar of your waterfalls;
all your waves and breakers
    have swept over me.

Leader: When you remember the good times with the Lord, do you now feel abandoned? Do the waters of chaos overwhelm you? Tell God about it.

(Pause.)

[8]By day the LORD directs his love,
    at night his song is with me—
    a prayer to the God of my life.

Leader: Make this verse your prayer now.

[9]I say to God my Rock,
    "Why have you forgotten me?
Why must I go about mourning,
    oppressed by the enemy?"

[10]My bones suffer mortal agony
    as my foes taunt me,
saying to me all day long,
    "Where is your God?"

Leader: The psalmist has seemingly made little progress in his quest for the presence of God. How much progress have you made? Tell God. Do you have friends who are more like enemies in taunting you about your faith? Lay them before the Lord.

[11]Why are you downcast, O my soul?
    Why so disturbed within me?
Put your hope in God,
    for I will yet praise him,
    my Savior and my God.

Leader: Here is the psalmist's refrain again. Meditate on its two poles— the present despair and the hope in God for relief.

[1]Vindicate me, O God,
    and plead my cause against an ungodly nation;
    rescue me from deceitful and wicked men.
[2]You are God my stronghold.
    Why have you rejected me?
Why must I go about mourning,
    oppressed by the enemy?

Leader: The psalmist again cries out to God, this time for his nation, his culture. Pray for your society, your enemies and the enemies of your culture at its best.

[3]Send forth your light and your truth,

let them guide me;
let them bring me to your holy mountain,
to the place where you dwell.

Leader: Ask God for his guidance through Scripture and your community of faith.
(Pause.)

4Then will I go to the altar of God,
to God, my joy and my delight.
I will praise you with the harp,
O God, my God.

Leader: In a minute we will be singing together. Prepare for this now as we all say together the final verse. As we say it, put your emphasis on the final three lines.

5Why are you downcast, O my soul?
Why so disturbed within me?
Put your hope in God,
for I will yet praise him,
my Savior and my God.

Leader: Let us sing together. (Choose a hymn or praise song that emphasizes hope for God's presence in our lives.)
Leader: How has the psalmist's experience and his prayer been helpful to you today?

SOME PARTING REMARKS

Share with the group the comments on prayer on page 105.

A Plea for Deliverance from Slander

Psalm 7

Sticks and stones will break your bones, but words will kill your spirit. That's not the common wisdom, of course, but it's true. Words have the power not only to lift the spirit and send it soaring but to sear the conscious mind, plunge beneath its protective rationality, invade the central chambers of the self and poison the soul. All of us have at one time learned that someone we know and love has broken a confidence, revealed an intimate detail, or gone behind our back to destroy our character with lies.

The villain Iago in Shakespeare's *Othello* was right about one thing, though he scarcely lived by his best lights.

> Who steals my purse steals trash; 'tis something, nothing;
> 'Twas mine, 'tis his, and has been slave to thousands;
> But he that filches from me my good name
> Robs me of that which not enriches him,
> And makes me poor indeed.

Plays on Broadway can close after one performance when the viperous pen of a vitriolic critic releases venom on the arts page of next morning's paper. Reputations are destroyed by gossip. Jobs are lost. Credibility lies in shambles.

What are honest men and women to do when this happens? Fight back? Return slander for slander? Or keep quiet? Often, so it seems to me, keeping quiet, making calm responses that may slowly put things right— these seem the better response. Jesus, for instance, did not reply to false accusations at his trial. When he was arrested, he told Peter to put away his sword. Of course, Jesus was on the way to the cross, and he had a mission to accomplish that prevented him from calling legions of angels to his side. But what should we do?

Psalm 7 presents for us one way David responded to such a situation. Scholars hesitate to say for certain what specific events are indicated by the phrase "concerning Cush the Benjaminite," but Cush may well have falsely accused David of treason. In any case, David has been seriously maligned and is fighting back, not by carrying his case before King Saul but by bringing it to God. Since Cush is never mentioned in any extant historical account, we know neither who he was nor how David responded to him either in public or private. We have, however, something better. We have David at prayer.

Before we attempt to pray David's very personal prayer, we need to empathize with David, to get inside his head and heart. That should help us discern how we might make David's words something of our own answering speech when we face a similar situation.

INITIAL READING OF PSALM 7

As with all the psalms we will pray, we start with multiple readings, some in silence, some aloud. We let the text present itself to us while we listen to its tone and tenor, attend to those words and phrases that pop out at us, and absorb its pattern of thought and emotion.

Psalm 7

A Shiggaion [musical form?] of David, which he sang to the LORD concerning Cush, a Benjaminite.

> ¹O LORD my God, in you I take refuge;
>> save me from all my pursuers, and deliver me,
> ²or like a lion they will tear me apart;
>> they will drag me away, with no one to rescue.
>
> ³O LORD my God, if I have done this,
>> if there is wrong in my hands,
> ⁴if I have repaid my ally with harm
>> or plundered my foe without cause,
> ⁵then let the enemy pursue and overtake me,
>> trample my life to the ground,
>> and lay my soul in the dust.
>
> *Selah*
>
> ⁶Rise up, O LORD, in your anger;
>> lift yourself up against the fury of my enemies;
>> awake, O my God; you have appointed a judgment.
> ⁷Let the assembly of the peoples be gathered around you,
>> and over it take your seat on high.
> ⁸The LORD judges the peoples;
>> judge me, O LORD, according to my righteousness,
>> and according to the integrity that is in me.

[9]O let the evil of the wicked come to an end,
>   but establish the righteous,
>   you who test the minds and hearts,
>   O righteous God.
[10]God is my shield,
>   who saves the upright in heart.
[11]God is a righteous judge,
>   and a God who has indignation every day.

[12]If one does not repent, God will whet his sword;
>   he has bent and strung his bow;
[13]he has prepared his deadly weapons,
>   making his arrows fiery shafts.
[14]See how they conceive evil,
>   and are pregnant with mischief,
>   and bring forth lies.
[15]They make a pit, digging it out,
>   and fall into the hole that they have made.
[16]Their mischief returns upon their own heads,
>   and on their own heads their violence descends.

[17]I will give to the LORD the thanks due to his righteousness,
>   and sing praise to the name of the LORD, the Most High.

GETTING AT THE MEANING OF PSALM 7

Other than the setting, which, while mentioned, remains obscure, the psalm is straightforward and poses few problems to our understanding. But it is important to understand the flow of ideas and their emotional counterparts.

Rational Structure

Plea for deliverance from slander

¹O LORD my God, in you I take refuge;
    save me from all my pursuers, and deliver me,
²or like a lion they will tear me apart;
    they will drag me away, with no one to rescue.

Declaration of innocence

³O LORD my God, if I have done this,
    if there is wrong in my hands,
⁴if I have repaid my ally with harm
    or plundered my foe without cause,
⁵then let the enemy pursue and overtake me,
    trample my life to the ground,
    and lay my soul in the dust.

Selah

Prayer for judgment of the slanderer

⁶Rise up, O LORD, in your anger;
    lift yourself up against the fury of my enemies;
    awake, O my God; you have appointed a judgment.
⁷Let the assembly of the peoples be gathered around you,
    and over it take your seat on high.
⁸The LORD judges the peoples;

Prayer for judgment of the psalmist to show his innocence

    judge me, O LORD, according to my righteousness,
    and according to the integrity that is in me.

Prayer for judgment for all the righteous

[9]O let the evil of the wicked come to an end,
    but establish the righteous,
you who test the minds and hearts,
    O righteous God.
[10]God is my shield,
    who saves the upright in heart.
[11]God is a righteous judge,
    and a God who has indignation every day.

Warning of coming judgment
[12]If one does not repent, God will whet his sword;
    he has bent and strung his bow;
[13]he has prepared his deadly weapons,
    making his arrows fiery shafts.

Judgment as self-destruction
[14]See how they conceive evil,
    and are pregnant with mischief,
    and bring forth lies.
[15]They make a pit, digging it out,
    and fall into the hole that they have made.
[16]Their mischief returns upon their own heads,
    and on their own heads their violence descends.

A resolution of thanks and praise for God's righteousness
[17]I will give to the LORD the thanks due to his righteousness,
    and sing praise to the name of the LORD, the Most High.

This outline makes the psalm look more rationally structured than it really is. David is disturbed, and the emotional turmoil he experiences spills out in his prayer. Thomas Merton says, "The Psalms are all made up of . . . cries of wonder, exultation, anguish or joy. The very concreteness of their passion makes some of them seem disjointed and senseless." Psalm 7 is not quite disjointed and senseless, but it is an intense cry with at least the sense of a certain answer.

Emotional Structure

David begins with an urgent plea for refuge, for safety from foes who would tear his flesh like lions. He has been accused, so it appears, of treason and has been threatened with dire consequences. He would gladly take the consequences if he had done what he is accused of, but, he says, he is utterly innocent of any wrongdoing. So he calls on God to arrest his accusers and bring them before the bar of righteous judgment. In his righteousness, David too will stand before the bar, confident and fearless.

David then pours forth his prayer for God in his righteous anger to punish the wicked and establish righteousness. He calls for people to repent and then pictures God as bending his bow to aim fiery shafts of judgment at those who are guilty before him.

We should notice here that David does not ask God for permission to wreak his own vengeance on his enemies. Nor does he ask God to forgive him for already doing so. Nor has he "shaken his fist in his pocket," as my grandfather used to urge me to do. Rather he calls on God, knowing that "vengeance is mine, I will repay, says the Lord" (Rom 12:19; see Prov 25:21-22).

David's vision of the self-destructive nature of evil is likewise graphic. The wicked *conceive* evil and lies are *born;* they dig pits and fall into them;

their mischief rebounds on them; they suffer from their own violence.

Then as quickly and dramatically as his prayer began, it ends. David has made his case, and that's it. God will answer. Only two things are left to do. First, he will give thanks to God, who, because of God's righteous character, he assumes will provide both refuge from present danger and judgment on his enemies. Second, he will sing praise to the most high Lord.

Can we pray this psalm as it is written? When we feel that we have been maligned, are we so sure of our innocence? Do we have the audacity to call on God to judge those who have done us wrong? We can try.

PRAYING PSALM 7

The guided prayer that follows assumes that as you pray you are responding to a betrayal by someone—perhaps a friend, perhaps not—and are still dealing with the emotional repercussions.

> [1]O LORD my God, in you I take refuge;
>> save me from all my pursuers, and deliver me,
> [2]or like a lion they will tear me apart;
>> they will drag me away, with no one to rescue.

Respond: *Lord, like the psalmist I flee to you for safety and refuge, not only from those who have wronged me but from my own anger and frustration. I fear what I might do if you do not save me both from him/her/them and from myself.* Tell God what the situation is. Name names. Express to God your anger with your "enemies." Pour out your heart.

> [3]O LORD my God, if I have done this,
>> if there is wrong in my hands,
> [4]if I have repaid my ally with harm
>> or plundered my foe without cause,

⁵then let the enemy pursue and overtake me,

>   trample my life to the ground,

>   and lay my soul in the dust.

Selah

Respond: Now clear your own conscience. *Lord, I do not believe I deserve the remarks made about me. I am innocent. But Lord, if there is something I do not know about my character or my actions, I lay myself bare before you. Show me my faults.*

Pause, to let God bring to mind any hidden factors in your receiving the critical remarks of others.

Forgive me of my secret sins—yes, even the sins I don't let myself know I have committed and am committing. I fear to say as David did, "Let my enemies trample my life to the ground and lay my soul in the dust." Lord, both forgive and forget my sin. But give me the grace to accept the consequences as you see fit. Still, Lord, bring judgment to my enemies as I do say with David:

⁶Rise up, O LORD, in your anger;

>   lift yourself up against the fury of my enemies;

>   awake, O my God; you have appointed a judgment.

⁷Let the assembly of the peoples be gathered around you,

>   and over it take your seat on high.

⁸The LORD judges the peoples;

>   judge me, O LORD, according to my righteousness,

>   and according to the integrity that is in me.

Respond: Picture a huge courtroom with God as judge, a great crowd assembled, the enemies in the dock, and the guilty among the people being brought up for judgment, then the psalmist arraigned and found not only not guilty but righteous. *O Lord, where am I among those arraigned—guilty or innocent? Can I be as righteous as David? Only by the blood of Christ. Cover me with*

the righteousness of my Lord Jesus Christ, and I shall stand in your court without fear
but with joy and exultation.

> [9]O let the evil of the wicked come to an end,
>> but establish the righteous,
> you who test the minds and hearts,
>> O righteous God.
> [10]God is my shield,
>> who saves the upright in heart.
> [11]God is a righteous judge,
>> and a God who has indignation every day.

Respond: *O Lord, do let the evil of the wicked come to an end. Establish justice. Establish justice not just for me in the face of my accusers but over all the earth.* Here list those people and places where you are especially conscious of injustice and evil. Pray for God's justice and mercy to prevail in concrete ways in our world today.

> [12]If one does not repent, God will whet his sword;
>> he has bent and strung his bow;
> [13]he has prepared his deadly weapons,
>> making his arrows fiery shafts.
> [14]See how they conceive evil,
>> and are pregnant with mischief,
>> and bring forth lies.
> [15]They make a pit, digging it out,
>> and fall into the hole that they have made.
> [16]Their mischief returns upon their own heads,
>> and on their own heads their violence descends.

Respond: *O Lord, I can't get the evil of the evil ones out of my mind. Like David, I see them self-destructing. On fields of battle I see them blown up by their own mines. In the boardrooms of corporations, I see their fraud turn their accounts to dust. In robberies, I see the weapons of thieves explode in their own hands. Stop my imagination, Lord. It's getting unhealthy for me. Let me rather praise you for your holy judgment.*

¹⁷I will give to the LORD the thanks due to his righteousness,
       and sing praise to the name of the LORD, the Most High.

Respond: *Thank you for your righteousness. Hallelujah!*

SOME FURTHER REFLECTIONS

I have interpreted this psalm as a response to slander. But it is generic enough in its treatment of this that it can be prayed in response to other acts of "enemies": those who cause us bodily harm, those who hurt our friends, those who tempt us to sin, to name a few.

Small Group Study of Psalm 7

The following comments are directed to the leader.

Introduction

Explain that Psalm 7 may deal with an issue that people in the group may not currently face but almost surely will at some time. So long as we are fallen humans on fallen earth, we will all be subject to our faults and foibles.

Group Instruction and Questions

1. Have one person read Psalm 7 in its entirety at an ordinary pace.

2. Before the second reading, explain that *concerning Cush, a Benjaminite* probably refers to a time before David was king. Cush had perhaps accused him of treason, and David feared for his life.

3. Have another person read Psalm 7 very slowly, with a pause after each verse.

4. Continue with a third reading.

5. Describe David's emotion as he begins this psalm (vv. 1-3). How troubled is he?

6. Assuming that this psalm (or prayer) involves Cush's having accused David of treason, what two things does David pray for (vv. 1-2)? (Protection from his enemies and the restoration of his good name.)

7. David is probably already high up in the government of Israel. So why do you think he is so intent on declaring himself innocent of Cush's charge?

   What is he willing to do to clear himself of Cush's slander (v. 8)?

8. How does David depict the working out of righteous judgment (vv. 5, 6-8, 12-13)?

9. What emotions are attributed to God (vv. 6, 11)?

   Why would he have *indignation every day?*

10. What do you think it would mean for God to *establish the righteous* today?

11. Given God's attitude toward evil and evildoers, what does David see as necessary for everyone to achieve righteousness (v. 12)?

12. Why do you think David returns again to a description of the wicked (vv. 14-16)?

    What new dimension do these verses add to how the wicked are judged?

13. Why is verse 17 a fitting, though sudden, end to the psalm?

DIRECTED PRAYER

The following script may help the group to pray the psalm.

Leader: Let us pray through Psalm 7. We'll say the first two verses together.

> ¹O LORD my God, in you I take refuge;
>> save me from all my pursuers, and deliver me,
> ²or like a lion they will tear me apart;
>> they will drag me away, with no one to rescue.

Leader: Consider these words we have just spoken. Do they reflect your experience now? Have you been slandered or falsely accused or subject of gossip? Are there troubles and troublemakers in your life today? Lay them before the Lord in silence.

(Pause.)

Reflect on your own role in the troubles you are recalling.

> ³O LORD my God, if I have done this,
>> if there is wrong in my hands,

⁴if I have repaid my ally with harm
>   or plundered my foe without cause,
⁵then let the enemy pursue and overtake me,
>   trample my life to the ground,
>   and lay my soul in the dust.

Selah

Leader: Are you willing to make these words your own? If not, confess your own culpability in the trouble.

(Pause.)

Then call on God:

⁶Rise up, O LORD, in your anger;
>   lift yourself up against the fury of my enemies;
>   awake, O my God; you have appointed a judgment.
⁷Let the assembly of the peoples be gathered around you,
>   and over it take your seat on high.
⁸The LORD judges the peoples;
>   judge me, O LORD, according to my righteousness,
>   and according to the integrity that is in me.

Leader: Self-reflect carefully here. Picture yourself in the courtroom with God as judge and you, your enemies and your community in the dock— the enemies first, your community second, and you last. Who can stand?

(Pause.)

⁹O let the evil of the wicked come to an end,
>   but establish the righteous,
> you who test the minds and hearts,
>   O righteous God.
¹⁰God is my shield,

who saves the upright in heart.

[11]God is a righteous judge,

and a God who has indignation every day.

Leader: Now picture your local world free of evil and characterized by righteousness. Can you do this? How hard is it? Why?

(Pause.)

[12]If one does not repent, God will whet his sword;

he has bent and strung his bow;

[13]he has prepared his deadly weapons,

making his arrows fiery shafts.

Leader: Remember, repentance is the doorway to being declared righteous. A change of character is the realization of that righteousness. Pray for the realization of righteousness in you and your community.

(Pause.)

[14]See how they conceive evil,

and are pregnant with mischief,

and bring forth lies.

[15]They make a pit, digging it out,

and fall into the hole that they have made.

[16]Their mischief returns upon their own heads,

and on their own heads their violence descends.

Leader: Take one last look at the wicked. Realize that the consequences of their evil will itself often be judgment enough. Slanderers will be slandered, though not by the righteous. Tell God that you are leaving to him the judgment of those who have slandered or troubled you.

(Pause.)

Now, let's say together the last verse and so indicate our own confidence that God will work his righteous judgment.

[17]I will give to the LORD the thanks due to his righteousness,
  and sing praise to the name of the LORD, the Most High.

Leader: Let us close with a song of praise.

SOME PARTING REMARKS

Personal injury such as slander and gossip can be deeply troubling. Be ready to listen to the lamentations of those in the group who feel that they have been set upon unjustly. The counsel of this psalm is to tell God about it and let him take care of the situation.

Of course, if there is something you can do to act as a go-between and help restore good relationships, be prepared to act as an agent of reconciliation.

SEVEN

A Blazing Song of Joy

Psalm 84

T he Pearl of the Psalms," Charles Spurgeon calls it. "No music could be too sweet for its theme, or too exquisite in sound to match the beauty of its language." Indeed, Spurgeon says, the psalmist "had a holy lovesickness upon him" as he longed for the presence of God. The result is one of the most glorious of the psalms. For us it will be a respite from the agonizing we have just experienced in Psalm 7 and a preparation for the awe-full horror we will encounter in Psalm 137.

There is something for everyone in Psalm 84. It combines the poignant, meditative beauty of poetry with an anticipation of ritual action. It glories in yearning for the presence of God, its pursuit and its realization.

INITIAL READING OF PSALM 84

Psalm 84
To the leader: according to The Gittith.
Of the Korahites. A Psalm.

[1]How lovely is your dwelling place,

O LORD of hosts!
²My soul longs, indeed it faints
     for the courts of the LORD;
my heart and my flesh sing for joy
     to the living God.

³Even the sparrow finds a home,
     and the swallow a nest for herself,
     where she may lay her young,
at your altars, O LORD of hosts,
     my King and my God.
⁴Happy are those who live in your house,
     ever singing your praise.   *Selah*

⁵Happy are those whose strength is in you,
     in whose heart are the highways to Zion.
⁶As they go through the valley of Baca
     they make it a place of springs;
     the early rain also covers it with pools.
⁷They go from strength to strength;
     the God of gods will be seen in Zion.

⁸O LORD God of hosts, hear my prayer;
     give ear, O God of Jacob!   *Selah*
⁹Behold our shield, O God;
     look on the face of your anointed.

¹⁰For a day in your courts is better
     than a thousand elsewhere.
I would rather be a doorkeeper in the house of my God
     than live in the tents of wickedness.

¹¹For the LORD God is a sun and shield;
    he bestows favor and honor.
  No good thing does the LORD withhold
    from those who walk uprightly.
¹²O LORD of hosts,
    happy is everyone who trusts in you.

Read and reread the psalm. Read it aloud. Read it silently. Absorb its language, feel its emotions, trace its flow.

GETTING AT THE MEANING OF PSALM 84

I want to confess what has concerned me in writing this book. As I indicate in the preface, my intention throughout is to encourage and help you to pray the psalms on your own. That means that you will be learning to do, and actually doing, the sort of careful preparation that I hope I am modeling in each of these chapters. Each chapter has essentially six stages:

1. intentional, intensive, quiet, meditative reading and absorption of the unmediated, direct language of each psalm

2. determination of the structure and flow of the ideas (rational structure)

3. determination and reflection on the emotional structure

4. recognition of the historical, cultural and intellectual background of the psalm, often through consulting the work of scholars

5. realization of the central character of the psalm

6. grasping the relevance of the psalm to you and your community, so that it can become part of your own answering speech to God

The problem is this: All my models do the bulk of the work for you.

How can you learn to do this work without going it on your own? Perhaps, I should simply end this chapter right here . . . Okay. I won't. But you get my point.

I will say, though, that most of the psalms I have already discussed have been with me for a long time. I have known them and prayed them casually and intently. The present psalm, however, is one with which I am less familiar. It has been good for me to include Psalm 84, because writing this chapter has reminded me of what must be done when one works largely from scratch. Perhaps such is the case for you: the psalms are all relatively new. In what follows I will trace some of my mental meanderings as I tried to come to grips with Psalm 84.

The heading of the psalm directs the liturgist to sing it *according to The Gittith*, that is, to a particular tune, or perhaps instrument, whose character is sweet or tender. Spurgeon suggests a tune "sweeter than the joy of the winepress." "The Korahites," says Marvin Tate, "are a guild of temple singers."

Rational Structure

It was not easy for me to see the rational structure of the psalm. It took several readings and even some suggestions from my two most helpful scholarly references to see what I now think is plain as the nose on Cyrano de Bergerac. The key was provided by seeing that this was a song of Zion, one reflecting on the longing of a pilgrim for the courts of the temple, the pilgrimage itself and the presence of God.

Actually, it is probably my experience that barricaded me from seeing the obvious, while my innate love of poetry broke that barrier. I was raised in a nonliturgical church. Singing, Bible reading, preaching and praying—that was the form of worship. Ritual was spare to nonexistent. But I have a deep love for artistic language, especially poetry. Some of the hymns we sang were great poetry—"A Mighty Fortress Is Our God" and "Fairest Lord Jesus," for example—and so is some of the Bible. The poetry of Psalm 84 was a great boon to my grasping the whole of this poem— surely one combining the arts of ritual and poetry. Here is the rational structure I have discovered.

The beauty of Zion
> ¹How lovely is your dwelling place,
>> O LORD of hosts!

Longing for Zion (the presence of God)
> ²My soul longs, indeed it faints
>> for the courts of the LORD;
> my heart and my flesh sing for joy
>> to the living God.

The hominess of Zion
> ³Even the sparrow finds a home,
>> and the swallow a nest for herself,
>> where she may lay her young,
> at your altars, O LORD of hosts,
>> my King and my God.

Joy in Zion
> ⁴Happy are those who live in your house,
>> ever singing your praise.   *Selah*

The joy of pilgrims to Zion
> ⁵Happy are those whose strength is in you,

in whose heart are the highways to Zion.
⁶As they go through the valley of Baca
they make it a place of springs;
the early rain also covers it with pools.
⁷They go from strength to strength;
the God of gods will be seen in Zion.

Refrain/invocation

⁸O LORD God of hosts, hear my prayer;
give ear, O God of Jacob!   *Selah*

The joy of servants in Zion

⁹Behold our shield, O God;
look on the face of your anointed.
¹⁰For a day in your courts is better
than a thousand elsewhere.
I would rather be a doorkeeper in the house of my God
than live in the tents of wickedness.

The God of Zion

¹¹For the LORD God is a sun and shield;
he bestows favor and honor.
No good thing does the LORD withhold
from those who walk uprightly.

The joy of all who trust in the God of Zion

¹²O LORD of hosts,
happy is everyone who trusts in you.

With careful reading, the overall structure of the psalm becomes clear. Think of an Israelite living somewhere outside Jerusalem, perhaps in the far north of Israel. He casts his mind toward Jerusalem, not just the city but the *dwelling place* of God (v. 1). This reflection elicits longing (v. 2) and triggers the vision of sparrows and swallows that make their home in the nooks and crannies of the temple, laying their eggs like gifts on the altar (v. 3). Suddenly the psalmist can't contain his emotion and exclaims: *Happy* are those who dwell in the temple! (v. 4).

Then shifting to a new theme, as if he has thought of something just as important, the psalmist exclaims again: *Happy* are those who make their pilgrimage to Zion! (v. 5). This is followed by a vision of pilgrims making their way through the desert with springs bubbling up, pools filling with rain, and the pilgrims getting stronger as they travel (vv. 6-7). The valley of Baca has not been identified, but it symbolizes a dry and thirsty land, now made fertile by God, one assumes, in the presence of the pilgrims.

Again there is a sudden exclamation as the spirit within the psalmist bursts its bounds: *O LORD God of hosts, hear my prayer* (v. 8). Notice that the psalmist has not asked for anything. His prayer is simply the exuberant anticipated joy of seeing pilgrims coming into the presence of God. He continues in this joyful mood as he calls on God to attend to the king (*our shield* and *the anointed*) and declares that true joy lies not in *the tents of wickedness* but in *the house of my God* (v. 10).

In the last strophe, Zion disappears and God alone commands the psalmist's attention, for God is *sun* (the light of life), *shield* (protector) and the giver of every good gift (v. 11).

Finally comes a fourth exclamation addressed to God: *Happy is everyone who trusts in you!* Note the progression: happy are the worshipers in the temple; happy are the pilgrims; happy is every worshiper in or out of the temple!

Rhetorical Structure

The psalmist alternates his address first to God, then to his fellow Israelite worshipers, then back and forth between them.

- to God: verses 1, 3-5, 8-10, 12
- to the Israelite worshipers: verses 2, 6-7, 11

It's as if we are overhearing the psalmist's prayer and receiving his commentary as well.

Emotional Structure

When poetry combines so beautifully with piety, "my heart leaps up," as William Wordsworth once said upon seeing a "host of golden daffodils." The psalmist's heart leaped for the vision of Zion. Inspired by the poetry, my heart too leaps up in anticipation of the presence of God.

Is there an emotion called "lovely"? Is it not love itself? Not *agape* love, the overflowing love of grace, but *romantic* love—to put it in sentimental terms, the intimate affection of a man and a woman. In any case, that is where this psalm begins: the love of the psalmist for the courts of the Lord, then the joy of the psalmist as he longs for the Lord (vv. 1-4). The psalmist is bringing to mind Zion, the temple sitting atop the high ridge of the City of David, the residence of the ark of the covenant, symbol of the very presence of God. There is little progress in this emotion, nor is there a sudden shift or dark moment. Rather, the emotional complex of love and joy goes from strength to strength, exploding in four direct addresses to God, moving from Zion as the place of God's dwelling to the presence of God, which, as every psalmist knew, is not the temple made by hands but wherever God chooses to make himself known.

A MODERN PARALLEL

Once Marj and I found ourselves in Piccadilly Circus in London. We had just come from a week of vacationing with our son Gene and his wife in a farmhouse converted to a small retreat center on the cliffs of southwest Wales. It had been a wonderful time of utter relaxation and refreshment—the natural beauty of the waves crashing hundreds of feet below us, the choughs hovering over windswept precipices, the rain pelting the roofs of the farmhouse, dovecote and outbuildings, the sun peeking out of wispy clouds.

Now we had only just entered London via the Tube, emerged from the darkness into an unusually sunny late afternoon, checked into our tiny hotel and were sitting on the open upper level of a big red London tour bus. Below us, in the gathering gloom of early evening, we were surrounded by examples of every strata of London life. As we looked down from our tourist perch, elegantly dressed men and women walked toward evening dinners in fine restaurants and theater shows, workers headed home from their posts as clerks at upscale and down-market stores, tourist families with kids of all ages strolled the streets, and young people with and without orange and green punk hair jostled their way through the crowds. In the midst of this hubbub, a dozen Hare Krishna worshipers came banging tambourines, dancing and chanting,

Hare Krishna, Hare Krishna,

Hare Hare, Krishna Krishna.

Not a single soul in this scene looked happy. Their faces were the faces of London Underground riders during Monday-morning rush hour—dull, expressionless, fearful of looking as if they were somebody; anonymous, distant, faces of the dead.

As the tour bus slowly pulled away and the din subsided, my daughter-in-law, this being her first time outside the United States, looked awestruck and aghast. Marj was depressed. I was amused at their response. This was typical downtown London on a Saturday. I had been there before.

The next morning Marj and I went to All Souls Church, one subway stop from Piccadilly Circus, across the street from the main studios of the BBC. The atmosphere was utterly opposite to that of the evening before. People streamed into the church from all over London, from all walks of life—professionals and workers, young and old, singles and families, international students and American tourists. Their faces were beaming. They were alive and expectant. They knew where they were going: they had just passed through the valley of Baca, the Piccadilly Circuses of London, and they had gone from strength to strength. The organ sounded, the formal service (actually quite informal for an Anglican service) began, the Word of God was read, hymns were sung, the Word was preached, prayers were lifted up. Life in Christ was celebrated. The congregation had come through the valley of Baca, entered Zion and for a few moments felt as if it was living in the presence of God, which it was.

PRAYING PSALM 84

I cannot emphasize enough the need to read and reread the psalm in preparation for prayer. This is not a mechanical exercise. Its goal is to internalize the psalm, to enter into its spirit, so that you can make it your answering speech. So read the psalm several times before you begin your prayer.

[1]How lovely is your dwelling place,
   O LORD of hosts!

Respond: *O Lord of hosts! Here I am thousands of years and thousands of miles away from the psalmist who penned those lines. The first temple is gone. Israel has gone into exile and come back, but it has never retrieved its glory. The second temple has been built and been destroyed. Only the Wailing Wall is left. Still, I feel at least in part the tender love these ancient lines represent. How lovely must have been the temple! How lovely these lines sound when they are sung in Brahms's* Requiem! *How lovely is any place you still appear! How lovely is our congregation, Lord, gathered on a Sunday morning to worship, to praise and to build fellowship with each other. We are a small part of your forever family still here on earth.*

> ²My soul longs, indeed it faints
>   for the courts of the LORD;
>   my heart and my flesh sing for joy
>   to the living God.

Respond: *Lord, it is you I long for, your presence I desire. For when you are near, when I get a sense of you as personal and direct, I am upheld by the knowledge that in Jesus Christ I can stand before you in a fear that is not terror, in a joyous awe in which my very flesh sings out wordless to you. I pause before you now, knowing that you are present.*
(Pause.)

> ³Even the sparrow finds a home,
>   and the swallow a nest for herself,
>   where she may lay her young,
> at your altars, O LORD of hosts,
>   my King and my God.

Respond: *We have sparrows, too, Lord. I imagine that they nest in the rafters of our church, for our church is a homey place. I am not thinking about our troubles as a congregation. They are nothing beside you and your presence. O my King and my God, rule my life as you rule your people! Rule our congregation as you rule your kingdom.*

⁴Happy are those who live in your house,
　　ever singing your praise.　　　　　　　　　*Selah*

Respond: *You have blessed us. You have blessed me. Hallelujah!*

⁵Happy are those whose strength is in you,
　　in whose heart are the highways to Zion.
⁶As they go through the valley of Baca
　　they make it a place of springs;
　　the early rain also covers it with pools.
⁷They go from strength to strength;
　　the God of gods will be seen in Zion.

Respond: *O God of gods and Lord of Lords, I see the pilgrims trekking through the wilderness. I see the valley of Baca, dry and desolate looming before them. I see springs of living water welling up in their path. I see the early, gentle spring rains, coursing down the once arid wadis and leaving pools in the low places. I see the pilgrims growing stronger and stronger, no longer merely trudging: their steps lighten as they anticipate your presence in Zion.*

⁸O LORD God of hosts, hear my prayer;
　　give ear, O God of Jacob!　　　　　　　　*Selah*

Respond: *Hear my prayer!*

⁹Behold our shield, O God;
　　look on the face of your anointed.

Respond: *We have no king to shield us. You, Lord, are our shield. Look on the face of each of us your children. Look on the face of our leaders—national and local. Name names. Look on my face, O Lord. But, as you did with Moses on the mountain, hide me in the cleft of a rock, shield me from the glory that would blind me. Yet be present to me as you, Father, were present to the disciples in Jesus.*

¹⁰For a day in your courts is better
    than a thousand elsewhere.
I would rather be a doorkeeper in the house of my God
    than live in the tents of wickedness.

Respond: *One day serving you is indeed better than a thousand in which I disobey and go my own way. Deliver me from temptation as you deliver me from evil.*

¹¹For the LORD God is a sun and shield;
    he bestows favor and honor.
No good thing does the LORD withhold
    from those who walk uprightly.

Respond: *You are the light of my life. You are my protector. You are the giver of every good gift. May I walk worthy of you!*

¹²O LORD of hosts,
    happy is everyone who trusts in you.

Respond: *O Lord of hosts, happy are your obedient people. Happy am I when I am in your will.*

SOME FURTHER REFLECTIONS

Two other songs of Zion—Psalms 46 and 137—are presented in this book. They form an interesting study in comparison and contrast.

Small Group Study of Psalm 84

The following comments are directed to the leader.

Introduction

This psalm should be a joy for the group to grasp and to pray. Open your study with a prayer that joy should blossom in your group.

Group Instructions and Questions

1. Have one person read Psalm 84 in its entirety at an ordinary pace.

2. Have another person read it very slowly, with a pause after each verse.

3. Read it a third time at a regular pace.

4. To get a response to the emotional or personal impact these readings have had, ask: What line or lines impressed you most? Why? (Take several answers from several participants.)

5. One literary critic used the phrase "feeling thought" to label the experience of powerful writing. How well or poorly does that help to describe your experience of reading and listening to this psalm? (You might have the group concentrate on the image of the birds building their nests in the temple. What does this mixing of the homey and the holy suggest about the psalmist's experience of God?)

6. What is the overall flow of ideas (the argument) in this psalm? (You may need to help participants notice the gradual progression from distant longing for Zion and God's presence [v. 1] to the reflection on God himself [vv. 11-12].)

7. Verses 5-7 depict the ancient pilgrims trekking through the arid desert as springs of water and early showers, harbingers of the rainy

season, leave pools of water. Does the psalmist's "feeling thought" (his experience) have any similarity to your experience of thinking about and attending your church's worship services, or some special interchurch gathering?

8. According the psalmist, who can be *happy* (blessed) and why?

9. Summarize the understanding of God that emerges when you consider the psalm as a whole.

When you believe the group is ready to make Psalm 84 their corporate prayer, proceed as directed.

DIRECTED PRAYER

The following script may help the group to pray the psalm.
Leader: Let us pray together verse 1:

> ¹How lovely is your dwelling place,
>   O LORD of hosts!

Leader: Imagine the magnificent temple sitting high atop the central mount in Jerusalem.
(Pause.)
Put yourself in the place of an ancient Hebrew living in the north of Israel and preparing in spirit for a pilgrimage.
(Pause.)
Now let's read together his longing reflection in verse 2.

> ²My soul longs, indeed it faints
>   for the courts of the LORD;
> my heart and my flesh sing for joy
>   to the living God.

(Pause. Then continue to read as leader.)

³Even the sparrow finds a home,
>   and the swallow a nest for herself,
>   where she may lay her young,
> at your altars, O LORD of hosts,
>   my King and my God.

Leader: Picture in your mind's eye the flitting sparrows, the darting swallows, the newly hatched young birds, the gentle homey spirit of the temple amidst its splendor.

(Pause.)

⁴Happy are those who live in your house,
>   ever singing your praise.   *Selah*

Leader: Blessed are those who then served in the temple. And blessed are those today who work among the congregation of believers and serve the church here and around the world!

⁵Happy are those whose strength is in you,
>   in whose heart are the highways to Zion.
⁶As they go through the valley of Baca
>   they make it a place of springs;
>   the early rain also covers it with pools.
⁷They go from strength to strength;
>   the God of gods will be seen in Zion.

Leader: But, Lord, even more blessed are those in whose hearts are the path to God, those who receive their strength from the indwelling of the Holy Spirit. Though they travel through hard places in their lives, you fill their needs and make their way a joy.

⁸O LORD God of hosts, hear my prayer;
    give ear, O God of Jacob!   *Selah*

Leader: Let's repeat that prayer together: O Lord God of hosts, hear my prayer; give ear, O God of Jacob!

⁹Behold our shield, O God;
    look on the face of your anointed.

Leader: Lord, we cannot ask for you to treat any of our leaders in the church or in our culture as if they were "anointed" like King David. But we can pray for your presence in the lives of those who have answered your call to become leaders in the community of believers or leaders in the business or political realm. May you look on them with favor! Here are those for whom we pray now . . . (Name names.)
    (Pause.)

¹⁰For a day in your courts is better
    than a thousand elsewhere.
  I would rather be a doorkeeper in the house of my God
    than live in the tents of wickedness.

Leader: Reflect on your desire to serve God.

¹¹For the LORD God is a sun and shield;
    he bestows favor and honor.
  No good thing does the LORD withhold
    from those who walk uprightly.

Leader: May we now acknowledge that the one sure way to be blessed is to put our trust in you. With the psalmist, we say together the final verse of this psalm:

[12]O LORD of hosts,

> happy is everyone who trusts in you.

Leader: Happy indeed! Amen.

SOME PARTING REMARKS

So many psalms, yet few are like Psalm 84, containing no darkness of anger, anxiety or memories of failure. Praise God for an island of joy in a sea of sadness!

Praying Our Anger
Psalm 137

We were living for a semester in Berkeley, my wife and I, when a phone call came from our daughter Ann, who had just begun college at Illinois Wesleyan, a two-hour drive from our permanent home in Downers Grove.

We talked about how we were enjoying our time in California. Then in a sad, lamenting voice, Ann asked, "Are you going to move to Berkeley?" I explained that I didn't know yet, but we liked Berkeley and, yes, we might move there someday.

"Are you going to sell the house?" she asked.

"Of course, we couldn't afford to move unless we did that," I replied, demonstrating my fatherly wisdom.

"Oh," she said, voice quivering, "it would be as if I'd never lived."

Three years later Ann went to Peru as a student for the summer. One year later, now a college graduate, she returned to Peru on her own, checking out the possibility of teaching English and continuing a relationship with a young man she had met the previous summer. Then after fifteen months living on her own as an English teacher, she returned to the States to teach Spanish. Soon she married a local fellow teacher. Now she, her husband and her two children live in Downers Grove, only a few blocks from the childhood home where her parents still live.

We are a people with a homing instinct. So were the Israelites in captivity in Babylon after the Babylonians destroyed Jerusalem in 587 B.C. We can understand their plaintive lament as they look back from Israel on that time spent in exile.

We have already seen how two psalmists (Ps 5 and 7) have called for God not only to deliver them from their enemies but also to judge and punish the guilty. But we have not yet seen the full depth of anger and revenge that some express as prophecies and curses. As C. S. Lewis says, "In some of the Psalms the spirit of hatred which strikes us in the face is like the heat from a furnace mouth." In Psalm 137 we see this anger at its briefest but most fevered pitch.

Wanting to pray the psalms by internalizing the profound spirituality of the psalms, we face a problem. Some parts of some psalms seem utterly inappropriate for Christians to pray. Here we will take up the challenge and deal with it head on. If we can appropriately pray Psalm 137, we can pray any other psalm, even those whose cursing is far more extensive.

INITIAL READING OF PSALM 137

Psalm 137

> ¹By the rivers of Babylon—
>> there we sat down and there we wept
>> when we remembered Zion.
> ²On the willows there
>> we hung up our harps.
> ³For there our captors
>> asked us for songs,
> and our tormentors asked for mirth, saying,

"Sing us one of the songs of Zion!"
⁴How could we sing the LORD's song
    in a foreign land?
⁵If I forget you, O Jerusalem,
    let my right hand wither!
⁶Let my tongue cling to the roof of my mouth,
    if I do not remember you,
 if I do not set Jerusalem
    above my highest joy.

⁷Remember, O LORD, against the Edomites
    the day of Jerusalem's fall,
 how they said, "Tear it down! Tear it down!
    Down to its foundations!"
⁸O daughter Babylon, you devastator!
    Happy shall they be who pay you back
    what you have done to us!
⁹Happy shall they be who take your little ones
    and dash them against the rock!

Read and reread this psalm until the flow of the words and your sense of the psalmist's emotions blend; then continue to read it until your emotions and those of the psalmist come close to being one. Now link those emotions with the intellectual content of the psalm. Do they match?

GETTING AT THE MEANING OF PSALM 137

Think back on your *first* reading of this psalm (not necessarily the first of the readings you've just finished). Do you recall your response to the final verse? If it was like mine, *shock!* would not be too strong to describe it. Even now I am horrified by the thought. Try as I might, I can't think that this brutal, vile slaughter of the innocent could ever be right. Then comes the immediate second thought. *How could this verse be in the Bible? Is God actually commending such violence?*

I expect that you, dear reader, are with me on this. Well, we can take at least some comfort in the fact that most scholars are with us as well. "Every line of it [the psalm]," Derek Kidner writes, "is alive with pain, whose intensity grows with each strophe to the appalling climax." Speaking in general about vengeance in the Psalms, Dietrich Bonhoeffer says, "No section of the Psalter causes us greater difficulty today than the so-called imprecatory psalms. With shocking frequency their thoughts penetrate the entire Psalter (5, 7, 9, 10, 13, 16, 21, 23, 28, 31, 35, 36, 40, 41, 44, 52, 54, 55, 58, 59, 68, 69, 70, 71, 137, and others). Every attempt to pray these psalms seems doomed to failure." Though they don't all say so, it is clear from their response that in their heart of hearts almost every scholar I consulted feels the same way. Their problem has been to explain not only why the line is in the psalm but why the psalm should have remained a part of the Christian biblical canon.

But we will not rush to answer this question. We should first be sure that we are responding not just to the final line but to the entire psalm.

Rational Structure

A situation remembered

¹By the rivers of Babylon—
>   there we sat down and there we wept
>   when we remembered Zion.
²On the willows there
>   we hung up our harps.
³For there our captors

asked us for songs,
and our tormentors asked for mirth, saying,
"Sing us one of the songs of Zion!"

Our response remembered

⁴How could we sing the LORD's song
in a foreign land?
⁵If I forget you, O Jerusalem,
let my right hand wither!
⁶Let my tongue cling to the roof of my mouth,
if I do not remember you,
if I do not set Jerusalem
above my highest joy.

A plea to God to remember injustice

⁷Remember, O LORD, against the Edomites
the day of Jerusalem's fall,
how they said, "Tear it down! Tear it down!
Down to its foundations!"

Prophecy (curse) addressed to Babylon

⁸O daughter Babylon, you devastator!
Happy shall they be who pay you back
what you have done to us!
⁹Happy shall they be who take your little ones
and dash them against the rock!

The flow of the argument is simple. A situation and response is re-
membered; a prophetic curse is delivered. There is little subtlety to the intellectual case against Babylon or to the punishment prophesied. There is,

however, much more subtlety to the moral and emotional structure.

The Moral and Emotional Structure

Rhetorically Psalm 137 is a marvel of emotional and moral structure.
The psalmist opens with a beautiful tableau:

> [1]By the rivers of Babylon—
>> there we sat down . . .

When I read this, I see a river flowing through a large oasis in the middle
of a vast city. I see the ancient Israelites sitting like the picnickers in Georges
Seurat's impressionist painting of elegant Parisians in the park on a Sunday
afternoon. Then I am brought up short by the next few words:

>> . . . and there we wept
>> when we remembered Zion.
> [2]On the willows there
>> we hung up our harps.

The beauty of the picture is enhanced as I see the harps hung on the
trees, but the emotion is changed from aesthetic appreciation to sympathy.
These are Jews from mountainous Jerusalem. These are exiles. And when
the psalmist goes on to explain why the harps are hung on the willows, the
emotions of his contemporary readers—those perhaps singing them as
lines in a liturgy—well up, as do mine, and my heart goes out to them:

> [3]For there our captors
>> asked us for songs,
> and our tormentors asked for mirth, saying,
>> "Sing us one of the songs of Zion!"

Was this taunting? Or was this like a slavemaster asking his slaves,
"Come up to the big house and sing your songs from Africa. Entertain

us"? In any case, it was deeply offensive to the Hebrews.

> ⁴How could we sing the LORD's song
>   in a foreign land?

Israel was their special home. They were God's people. The land of Israel was given to them by God. They were not supposed to be in Babylon. Jerusalem was Zion, the place where God dwelled. When this psalm was written the Israelites were back in Israel, to be sure, but the memory of their exile was still with them. They never, ever, ever wanted to forget Jerusalem, no matter what happened to them in the coming days and years.

> ⁵If I forget you, O Jerusalem,
>   let my right hand wither!
> ⁶Let my tongue cling to the roof of my mouth,
>   if I do not remember you,
>   if I do not set Jerusalem
>   above my highest joy.

The power of the images—the *withered hand*, the *parched tongue*—helps me see their plight more clearly. As a reader I am ready for the charge against Babylon, perhaps even for its rhetorical power.

> ⁷Remember, O LORD, against the Edomites
>   the day of Jerusalem's fall,
>   how they said, "Tear it down! Tear it down!
>   Down to its foundations!"

Maybe the only readers who can appreciate the rising anger of the psalmist are those whose city or house has been devastated by war or terrorism. This is, of course, a huge and growing number of people, as violent conflicts increase in our own post-9/11 world. Think of our anger here in the United States after that catastrophic event. Think of the anger of the Palestinians as their homes are confiscated by the Israelis. Or the anger of the Iraqis as they see their country blown up by foreign armies.

Of course the Hebrews thought the destruction of Jerusalem was unjust. It was not just their city but the temple of the one Living God. Naturally they called on God to right the wrong. Here the psalmist addresses the oppressor:

⁸O daughter Babylon, you devastator!

Then he envisions the fortune of those who will return punishment for evil—*lex talionis*, payment in kind.

Happy shall they be who pay you back
   what you have done to us!
⁹Happy shall they be who take your little ones
   and dash them against the rock!

We can take the payment in kind. That appeals to our primal sense of justice. I think of Mel Gibson's film *The Passion of the Christ* and remember the growing glee with which the Roman soldiers beat Jesus. I can understand the desire to see these same soldiers under the whip of men like them. Whatever we might think, or think we ought to think, wouldn't we all in our heart say, *It serves them right?*

But the final line is different. We can't pray that. We can hardly say it. Echoing in our mind are Jesus' words: "Let the little children come to me; do not stop them; for it is to such as these that the kingdom of God belongs" (Mk 10:14). Then we recall as well that *lex talionis* is inappropriate. "Do not repay evil for evil or abuse for abuse; but, on the contrary, repay with a blessing" (1 Pet 3:9), wrote Peter, echoing his Master's words, "Love your enemies and pray for those who persecute you" (Mt 5:44). In short, something seems to have gone wildly wrong for the psalmist to end his psalm at the peak of his anger with these awe-full, awful words.

IMPRECATION IN THE PSALMS

As Bonhoeffer noted, the theme of imprecation—cursing, calling down God's vengeance on evildoers—permeates the Psalter. If we sweep it under the hermeneutic rug, we will trip over it every time we kneel to pray. We have already dealt with its presence in Psalms 5 and 7. But consider the following passages as well.

The first, from Psalm 109, is a set of curses that David is either hurling against his enemies or, as the NRSV has it, quoting from his enemies against himself. In the latter case, David turns to God and says, in effect, Let all those curses on me be turned back on my enemies (v. 20). So they may just as well have been made by David in the first place:

> [6]. . . Appoint a wicked man against him:
>   let an accuser stand on his right.
> [7]When he is tried, let him be found guilty;
>   let his prayer be counted as sin.
> [8]May his days be few;
>   may another seize his position.
> [9]May his children be orphans,
>   and his wife a widow.
> [10]May his children wander about and beg;
>   may they be driven out of the ruins they inhabit.
> [11]May the creditor seize all that he has;
>   may strangers plunder the fruits of his toil.
> [12]May there be no one to do him a kindness,
>   nor anyone to pity his orphaned children.

[13]May his posterity be cut off;

> may his name be blotted out in the second generation.

The curses continue for six more verses! Here are other curses. From Psalm 10:

[15]Break the arm of the wicked and evildoers;

> seek out their wickedness until you find none.

From Psalm 28:

[4]Repay [the wicked] according to their work,

> and according to the evil of their deeds;

repay them according to the work of their hands;

> render them their due reward.

From Psalm 31:

[17]. . . Let the wicked be put to shame;

> let them go dumbfounded to Sheol.

[18]Let the lying lips be stilled

> that speak insolently against the righteous
>
> with pride and contempt.

From Psalm 58:

[6]O God, break the teeth in their mouths;

> tear out the fangs of the young lions, O LORD!

[7]Let them vanish like water that runs away;

> like grass let them be trodden down and wither.

[8]Let them be like the snail that dissolves into slime;

> like the untimely birth that never sees the sun.

[9]Sooner than your pots can feel the heat of thorns,

whether green or ablaze, may he sweep them away!

From Psalm 69:

[22]Let their table be a trap for them,
   a snare for their allies.
[23]Let their eyes be darkened so that they cannot see,
   and make their loins tremble continually.
[24]Pour out your indignation upon them,
   and let your burning anger overtake them.
[25]May their camp be a desolation;
   let no one live in their tents.
[26]For they persecute those whom you have struck down,
   and those whom you have wounded, they attack still more.
[27]Add guilt to their guilt;
   may they have no acquittal from you.
[28]Let them be blotted out of the book of the living;
   let them not be enrolled among the righteous.

Fellow prayers of the psalms, must we not find some way to deal with these passages so that the psalms in which they are embedded can still become our answering speech to God? "Houston," a *Columbia* astronaut said to ground control, "we have a problem." So do we.

WHAT THE SCHOLARS SAY

Scholars who face this problem squarely offer a network of explanations, most of which dovetail, so that while the emotional problem does not go completely away, at least the rational problem is largely answered. Here in order of their priority and importance are six factors that enter into an answer.

The Holiness of God

The most important factor is a notion foundational to Christian faith: *God is holy—utterly, absolutely, time-out-of-mind holy.* Christians constantly affirm this in private prayer, liturgy, preaching and teaching. But the fact is that most of us just don't get it. God is so holy, so set apart from us, that his nature is obscured and hidden, except where he wishes it to be revealed. Then whatever he reveals about the just, the true and the good is in fact the just, the true and the good. It is not that his character is whatever he declares it to be because he is free to be whatever he chooses. Rather, whatever he declares or reveals it to be is what it intrinsically is. From our standpoint, of course, we can never judge God. What we know of him is only what he reveals. The very categories (or criteria) we employ in our knowing are those he has given us. So is our ability to think and know. If our notion of what God should be is different from what he reveals himself to be in Scripture, we haven't a leg to stand on. God is God. Period.

If vengeance is to be done against those who have dishonored God or have acted unjustly against his people or his natural creation, God will do it. The psalmists universally assume this. They do not ask God for permission to wreak vengeance themselves. "Vengeance is mine, I will repay, says the Lord," says Paul (Rom 12:19), quoting Leviticus 19:18. The Old and New Testaments agree: vengeance is the business of God.

In Psalm 137, in fact, the psalmist does not really curse the Babylonians; he only prophesies the way vengeance will be delivered. This, of course, does not solve our dilemma as modern readers, for now it is God who will be responsible for the brutal action of Psalm 137:9 should this prophecy be fulfilled. This actually heightens our horror. How this vengeance is finally administered becomes evident only on the cross.

The Wickedness of Humankind

The corollary of God's holiness is our wickedness. This is everywhere assumed and often stated in Scripture, both the Old and New Testaments, as strikingly evident in Romans 3:9-18. In this section—a diatribe against human nature—Paul quotes from Psalms 5, 7, 14, 36 and 140 and from Isaiah 59. Paul universalizes these descriptions of the wicked, concluding: "All have sinned and fall short of the glory of God" (Rom 3:23). James echoes this universally negative take on human nature: "For whoever keeps the whole law but fails in one point has become accountable for all of it. For the one who said, 'You shall not commit adultery,' also said, 'You shall not murder'" (Jas 2:10-11).

Here is the crux of the matter. It is not just that a sinner has broken a law and thus stands abstractly guilty before that law. Rather, the crux of the matter is the violation of the proper relationship between the Lawgiver and the ones for whom the law was given. The sinner is not just a lawbreaker but a relationship breaker, a rebel.

The Justice of God's Judgment

When the relationship breaker finds himself or herself apart from God, the judgment has already begun. The major effect of that broken relationship is the multiple broken relationships—the internal ones within each individual and the external ones between individual men and women and among different communities, societies and nations. Wickedness runs rampant in society, kept in restraint only by the grace of God. The broken relationship between any person and God is made permanent if the relationship is not restored, and that can be done only by God himself at the cost of the incarnate Son of God, who experienced for all time and for all people his own separation from the Father. "My God, my God, why have you forsaken me?" Jesus cried from the cross, quoting the opening line of Psalm 22.

Calls for God's vengeance, then, are set within the theological context of the holiness of God and the wickedness of human beings. They are calls to realize in the context of space and time God's just and eternal judgment on desperately sinful people.

The Context of Ancient Israel

The historical context in which these imprecatory passages emerge can lessen the horror we feel when we read them today. First, for example, is the specific context of Psalm 137. The psalmist is remembering what took place when Israel was in exile. How did they get there? By the destruction of Jerusalem—a brutal invasion by the Babylonians with, it would seem, some collusion with the Edomites.

Dashing children against rocks was not at all unusual. It was, says Allen, "a feature of ancient Near Eastern warfare." For a poetic and emotional picture of the violence to the residents of Jerusalem, see Lamentations. Here, of course, God is seen as the one who is using Babylon to judge the Israelites for their sin. But this picture bears resemblance to the image in the last line of Psalm 137. For example, Lamentations 2:20-21:

> [20]Look, O LORD, and consider!
>> To whom have you done this?
>> Should women eat their offspring,
>>> the children they have borne?
>> Should priest and prophet be killed
>>> in the sanctuary of the Lord?
>
> [21]The young and the old are lying
>> on the ground in the streets;
>> my young women and my young men
>>> have fallen by the sword;

in the day of your anger you have killed them,
    slaughtering without mercy.

Jeremiah later prophesies that God will punish Babylon for its iniquity in much the same way as the psalmist envisions in Psalm 137 (Lam 3:55-63; Jer 25:12). From this perspective, *lex talionis* would seem to justify the punishment of Babylon. Of course, *lex talionis* is rejected by the Bible as a justification.

Second, also important for our grasp of the historical context of Psalm 137 is Israel's sense of its own destiny. The Israelites saw themselves as God's people. They were on a mission for God. Now they are in captivity. There is both the longing for home and the longing to fulfill their destiny. How can they do it here? How can they forget Zion? How can they sing the songs of Zion? How can they sing these utterly joyous songs, like Psalm 84, extolling the beauty and glory of the temple?

¹How lovely is your dwelling place,
        O LORD of hosts!
²My soul longs, indeed it faints
        for the courts of the LORD;
    my heart and my flesh sing for joy
        to the living God.

³Even the sparrow finds a home,
        and the swallow a nest for herself,
        where she may lay her young,
    at your altars, O LORD of hosts,
        my King and my God.
⁴Happy are those who live in your house,
        ever singing your praise.

The psalmist of this song of Zion "would rather be a doorkeeper in the house of my God than live in the tents of wickedness" (v. 10). And here the Israelites are in Babylon, living among, if not in, those very tents.

The pain is too great. They hang up their harps. Anger rises up as they respond to their captors' taunts and calls for entertainment. Now years later, as the psalmist reflects on this scene, his anger rises, and out comes the prophetic curse: "Happy shall they be who take your little ones and dash them against the rock!"

But it isn't just the memory of captivity that forms the background of Psalm 137. After the fall of Jerusalem in 587 B.C., even after the return of the Jews to the Holy Land, Israel was never more than a vassal state. The psalmist has only hope for the return of Jerusalem to its high status. In some ways the vision of revenge looks an idle threat, given in the heat of the moment. Was the prophecy ever carried out? To be sure, Babylon is no more—it has not existed for a couple of millennia or more. In the first century it became for Christians a symbol for Rome and all that was evil in the religious and political realm. But by then the city and its state had long been laid to waste.

Third, we need to remember that the psalmist did not know how God was going to solve the problem of evil and wickedness. Many of the psalmists may well have envisioned a messiah who would effect the final solution, but they had to look forward with vision, not backward with certainty. If all the psalmists could do was to call on God to avenge evil and to see this in brutal terms, it is at least a confirmation that they had not lost hope. God would bring justice. The question was only "How long, O Lord? How long?" The New Testament tells us.

A New Testament Perspective

We first need to set the New Testament treatment of vengeance in the context of the Old Testament. As already mentioned, Jesus and the apostles are at one concerning loving and doing good for one's enemies, that is, returning good for evil: "You have heard that it was said, 'You shall love your neighbor and hate your enemy.' But I say to you, Love your enemies and pray for those who persecute you, so that you may be children of your Father in heaven. . . . Be perfect, therefore, as your heavenly Father is perfect" (Mt 5:43-45, 48).

But this is not really a new teaching. Its root springs from the ancient Hebrew Scriptures.

> You shall not hate in your heart anyone of your kin; you shall reprove your neighbor, or you will incur guilt yourself. You shall not take vengeance or bear a grudge against any of your people, but you shall love your neighbor as yourself. (Lev 19:17-18)

> Do not rejoice when your enemies fall,
>   and do not let your heart be glad when they stumble,
> or else the LORD will see it and be displeased,
>   and turn away his anger from them. (Prov 24:17-18)

In other words, let God be the one to judge as he sees fit. Indeed there is vengeance, but it is God's business, not ours. We are not even to enjoy it.

Then too, judgment and the working out of God's wrath against evil and evildoers is by no means missing from the New Testament. Jesus' parables often end with judgment, and as he prophesies his own second coming, he explicitly speaks of separating the sheep from the goats, vividly depicting God's judgment: "You that are accursed, depart from me into the eternal fire prepared for the devil and his angels" (Mt 25:41). Not everyone will enter the kingdom of heaven, Jesus says, "only the one who does the will of my Father." The judgment is stern: "On that day many will say to me, 'Lord, Lord, did we not prophesy in your name, and cast out demons in your name, and do many deeds of power in your name?' Then I will declare to them, 'I never knew you; go away from me, you evildoers'" (Mt 7:22-23).

To top it off, Revelation 18 pictures the violent judgment of apocalyptic Babylon, the city of Satan and evil humanity.

Kidner sums up the "occasional equivalent of cursing in the New Testament":

> The Lord Himself led the way with His acted and spoken oracles of judgment on the unfruitful Israel (Mk. 11:14; 12:9) and on the unfaithful churches (Rev. 2f). In the age of the apostles, if the fate of Ananias and Sapphira was not actually invoked, the temporary blinding of Elymas was; so too was the handing over of the Corinthian offender to Satan (I Cor. 5:5).

Still, in both the Old and especially the New Testaments, the overwhelming picture we get of God is not as Judge but as Redeemer. He is the One who through the Son stands in our place before the high and holy bar of God's justice. God is both judge and sacrifice. The Son of God is dashed against the hard rock of Golgotha. He says, "My God, my God, why have you forsaken me?" (Mt 27:46). But when the Son is raised from the dead, we know the final conflict between good and evil is over: Righteousness and peace have kissed each other (Ps 85:10). The rest of history is a mop-up action, a bloody one, but one for which the end is certain.

The Context of Human Nature

Finally, let us note the profound realism of the psalms. From the joyous, exuberant praise of the glorious living God to the agonized frustration and fury of the unjustly accused; from the thankful spirit of the penitent sinner to the righteous indignation of the defender of God's people; from the quiet confidence of the sheep who love their Shepherd to the stinging vengeance of the one who desires the righting of all wrongs—the Psalter is realistic, sometimes it seems almost to a fault, as it leads us across the contours of human life.

The curses that proceed from the mouth of the psalmist are painfully true to human nature. Even when we are horrified by the expressions we read, we know that, faced with the same situations, we could say the same thing, even in our guarded moments, and have probably done so. It is this utter realism about human nature that is, I think, the key to how we are to pray these psalms.

IMPLICATIONS FOR PRAYING THE IMPRECATORY PSALMS

I have struggled with the imprecatory character of the psalms for many years. Off and on, I have come to terms with them, concluding that one or another way of understanding their place in the canon has solved their enigma. I believe that I have reached an understanding again, but I am not so certain I am correct as to urge my solution on you, my readers. Still, based on the six factors just discussed, I offer what I can.

First, when we turn to prayer from our absorption and study of the psalm, we can trust the psalmist not to mislead us into a prayer that in the final analysis would be incorrect to pray. If we find ourselves in the position of the psalmist, what else should we do but pour out the agony of our heart to God? If it comes out as a curse, it does so because that is what is in us crying out to be expressed. If we hate our enemy—or even, God forbid, our neighbor—God already knows it. We will not shock him. Lewis may be theologically right when he says, "The reaction of the Psalmists to injury, though profoundly natural, is profoundly wrong." But I think he is pastorally wrong. If we bottle up what we feel, we pay the consequences of its coming out in personally and socially far more destructive ways than as curses expressed to God in prayer. As Eugene Peterson wisely says, "Our hate needs to be prayed, not suppressed." It is safe to tell God absolutely anything. He already knows. And now *we* know: our hatred is now open to ourselves and God. And we can tell him what we think he ought to do—yes, be audacious. Plead with him as we will, he will never do what is wrong.

In this process God may change our heart. He may show us on the nerve endings of our life that we are railing at the wrong people, that we will be a better person if we stop it. And the Holy Spirit may transform us so that our perspective and our heart's desire is more like that of Jesus.

We must not glory in imprecation, trying to curse our and God's enemies with ever more clever language. Our spirit must be calmed and healed so that we do indeed return cursing with blessing, as did our Lord when he said, "Father, forgive them; for they do not know what they are doing" (Lk 23:34).

So much for our prayers in private. Except as direct quotations from the psalms, I am far less sure that we should include curses in our communal prayers. To spread our anger to others, even others whose emotions are similar to ours, may raise temptations to take vengeance into our own hands. The community of faith is not so safe as God.

And we must never ever speak them abroad! To stand in the marketplace—literally, or on radio or television or in print—and curse our enemies is disastrous. The reactions either with us or against us are likely to be socially destructive. If they are not violent, they still spread the venom of ill will and may lead to violence later.

But true spirituality is true to our broken nature. It derives not from perfect prayer but from honest prayer. We dare not lie to God! He will deal with our imperfection and by the power of the Holy Spirit heal our broken soul and restore us to himself. In the midst of honest, angry prayer, we can be confident that there is running in the background the concomitant prayer.

Second, we need intellectually to realize that Jesus put away all vengeance toward others when he died on the cross for their—for our—sin. Bonhoeffer captures the right way to proceed:

> Only in the cross of Jesus Christ is the love of God to be found.
>
> Thus the imprecatory psalm leads to the cross of Jesus and to the love of God which forgives enemies. I cannot forgive the enemies of God out of my own resources. Only the crucified Christ can do that, and I through him. Thus the carrying out of vengeance becomes grace for all men in Jesus Christ. . . . I leave the vengeance to God and ask him to execute his righteousness to all his enemies, knowing that God has remained in his wrathful judgment on the cross, and that this wrath has become grace and joy for us. Jesus Christ himself requests the execution of the wrath of God on his body, and thus he leads me back daily to the gravity and the grace of his cross for me and all enemies of God.
>
> Even today I can believe the love of God and forgive my enemies only by going back to the cross of Christ, to the carrying out of the wrath of God. The cross of Jesus is valid for all men. Whoever opposes him, whoever corrupts the word of the cross of Jesus on which God's wrath must be executed, must bear the curse of God some time or another. The New Testament speaks with great clarity concerning this and does not distinguish itself at all in this respect from the Old Testament, but it also speaks of the joy of the church in that day on which God will execute his final judgment (Galatians 1:8f; I Corinthians 16:22; Revelation 18; 19; 20:11). In this way the crucified Jesus teaches us to pray the im-

precatory psalms correctly.

Finally, the bottom line. One of the most important conclusions we can reach is this: If we are honest with ourselves, we can say anything to God. He can take it. We can call on him to do whatever violent or mischievous thing we can imagine. Why? Because we can trust him not to do what is wrong, even if we ask it in all sincerity. He will not do evil. The vengeance that is his is utterly—absolutely, time out of mind—just.

ANALOGICAL READING

When we read Psalm 137 we have no difficulty in understanding the situation out of which the psalm came nor the human emotions of the psalmist. Human nature has not changed. What is different, however, is that the specific events that triggered the psalm and its awe-full prophetic close are not ones that fit most of us today. We are indeed God's chosen people but not quite in the sense of the ancient Jews.

Moreover, we find the specific imprecatory close to the psalm too brutal and too foreign to us. If we are to make the psalm our answering speech, we will have to make some adjustments. I suggest that there are two parts to this process. The first is to understand the psalm in its own context and enter empathically into that context—that is, to understand it from the inside. This will, in my suggestion, mean praying the psalm as if we were the psalmist.

The second part of the process is to have so absorbed the mindset of the psalmist, so put it in the larger context of the cross, and so grasped its inner soul that it begins to resonate with our own concerns and our problems. Every modern Christian reader's or Christian community's specific issues and problems are different. In the directed prayer below I have assumed a problem that I believe to be common to many Christians: the tension in our lives brought on by the clash between the kingdom of God and the kingdom of this world.

PRAYING PSALM 137

Read through Psalm 137 again to refresh your memory of the flow of ideas. Read it again to re-sense its emotional flow.

Praying Psalm 137 will from here on be somewhat different from praying the other psalms we have so far prayed. We cannot easily make the psalmist's words our own unless we have been political or religious exiles. We will need to pray our prayer by analogy—finding in the experience of the exiles and the memory of the psalmist analogies to our own experience. So our procedure will be in two stages.

Stage One

Read through the entire psalm slowly, putting yourself imaginatively in the position of the psalmist and the Israelites in Babylon. Then pray:

Father, let me see and feel something of the plight of your chosen people away from the center of your plan for them, longing to return. Take me deeper into their experience through this distorted Song of Zion.

Now pray the entire psalm (out loud may be very helpful) as if you were the psalmist. Absorb as best you can the experience he transmits through the psalm. One warning: Do not try to reach the fever pitch of the last line. But do try to feel the pain of the psalmist as he calls down vengeance on the unjust.

Stage Two

Then with eyes open, pray through the psalm again section by section.

¹By the rivers of Babylon—
    there we sat down and there we wept
    when we remembered Zion.
²On the willows there
    we hung up our harps.
³For there our captors
    asked us for songs,
and our tormentors asked for mirth, saying,
    "Sing us one of the songs of Zion!"

Respond: *Lord, as I contemplate this scene and imaginatively feel the sorrow and yearning of the Israelites, I see myself and my community in the midst of our own hostile world. We Christians are like exiles, living in a country and a city that is foreign to our hearts when they are set on you. Of course we have never lived in Zion. We look forward to the time when we will, but we are not yet there. We have never lived in a city or worshiped in a church that fully met the ache in our heart for a final home. We have hymns to sing, and we have sung them with great gusto and great feeling. But the world wants entertainment, not worship of you, the one holy God. We cannot sing our songs of Zion for the titillation of those who are not your children. We would rather leave our organs unplayed, our piano shut, our guitars in their cases.*

⁴How could we sing the LORD's song
    in a foreign land?
⁵If I forget you, O Jerusalem,
    let my right hand wither!
⁶Let my tongue cling to the roof of my mouth,
    if I do not remember you,
if I do not set Jerusalem
    above my highest joy.

Respond: *We have not forgotten Zion; we have never really known it. We long for what we have never had. Never let us forget that we were made for another country— the kingdom of God, a kingdom of the Spirit that is more solid and real than the kingdom of this world. May life with you and your forever family be my deepest hope and my fondest joy.*

In your own context, lay before God your most intimate and deep desires, those that you know will lead you to a deeper life with God and a greater service to your community and the world. List what is standing in your way. Name the "demons" that are keeping you from a fuller Christian life.

> [7]Remember, O LORD, against the Edomites
>   the day of Jerusalem's fall,
> how they said, "Tear it down! Tear it down!
>   Down to its foundations!"

Respond: *Lord, I hear the voices of the world: "Tear down the church! Tear it down to the ground! Build up the kingdom of this world. Give us more money! Give us more stuff! Give me a bigger TV, a swimming pool, a water park in my own backyard! Take away the restraints on my freedom! Give me greater sex with more and more people! Give me . . . Give me . . . Give me more power, more control over others! Give me everything I want! . . . Do it now! Now! NOW!"* Name the barriers that keep you from living your life in light of the kingdom of God. If they were to speak, what would they say? Would they whisper or yell?

> [8]O daughter Babylon, you devastator!

Respond: *O Satan, you destroyer!* Renounce the challenges to your desire to live for God.

> Happy shall they be who pay you back

what you have done to us!

⁹Happy shall they be who take your little ones

and dash them against the rock!

Respond: *Blessed will be the day when you, O Satan, you great tempter, will be cast into utter darkness! Blessed will be the Lord in that great judgment day! And blessed will be your children, delivered from the kingdom of this world into the kingdom of your Son!* Rejoice in the day when the "demons" that tyrannize you will be destroyed.

Small Group Study of Psalm 137

The following comments are directed to the leader.

Introduction

This psalm is short but troubling. It's hard to imagine just what the reaction will be to the final verse. Be prepared to struggle with the group for an understanding that will allow fruitful prayer to emerge.

Group Instruction and Questions

1. Have one person read Psalm 137 in its entirety at an ordinary pace. Do not let conversation about verse 9 erupt, but continue with two more readings.

2. Have another person read it very slowly, with a pause after each verse.

3. A third reading would be helpful.

4. What strikes you about this psalm? Why? (There will probably be no way to keep the content of verse 9 from being the immediate topic of discussion. Keep that conversation as low key as possible so that real understanding can emerge.)

5. The final verse is, of course, shocking. What is the situation that gave rise to the curse? In other words, summarize the flow of ideas. (Some in the group may not be familiar with the historical situation assumed by the psalm. Have someone who does explain this. See pages 157-59 above for the basic details. Do not discuss whether the final verse is justified until you deal with question 6, involving the emotions.)

6. Have someone summarize the emotional flow—where it begins, how it increases and why it ends as it does.

How true to human nature is this emotional flow?

7. We can understand why the emotion rose to a fever pitch. We can see its connection to the history of Israel, but does the historical situation justify the psalmist's final curse? Why or why not? (At this point in may be necessary for the leader to present the material on imprecation, pages 154-65 above. This can be done while reading one section at a time, pausing for questions, and ensuring that most of the participants have understood the issues, whether they agree with the presentation or not. During the course of this presentation, be sure to include answers to question 8, which follows.)

8. What relevance do the following have to how we understand and feel about the imprecation in the psalms?

- the holiness of God
- the wickedness of human beings
- the justice of God's justice
- the history of Israel
- the biblical rejection of *lex talionis*
- returning good for evil, blessing for curses
- the crucifixion and resurrection of Jesus
- the presence and the coming of the kingdom of God

9. Ask each of the participants to explain whether they feel able to put themselves in the position of the psalmist and pray the psalm as if they were he. Those who do not wish to do so should not do so during the prayer time that follows. Tell them that they need not feel pressured to do it.

When you believe the group is ready to make Psalm 137 their corporate prayer, proceed as directed.

DIRECTED PRAYER

The following script may help the group to pray the psalm.

> ¹By the rivers of Babylon—
>> there we sat down and there we wept
>> when we remembered Zion.
> ²On the willows there
>> we hung up our harps.
> ³For there our captors
>> asked us for songs,
> and our tormentors asked for mirth, saying,
>> "Sing us one of the songs of Zion!"

Leader: Picture this scene in your mind.

(Pause.)

Leader: Imagine yourself in the scene as an Israeli in exile. How do you feel as a captive in a foreign land so different from your own, topographically, culturally, religiously?

(Pause.)

> ⁴How could we sing the LORD's song
>> in a foreign land?

Leader: What would it be like to sing the songs of Zion for the entertainment of your captors?

> ⁵If I forget you, O Jerusalem,
>> let my right hand wither!
> ⁶Let my tongue cling to the roof of my mouth,
>> if I do not remember you,
> if I do not set Jerusalem
>> above my highest joy.

Leader: What do you miss about Jerusalem? What do you miss when you are away from home? If you could never go back, would it have been as if you'd never lived?

(Pause.)

> [7]Remember, O LORD, against the Edomites
> the day of Jerusalem's fall,
> how they said, "Tear it down! Tear it down!
> Down to its foundations!"

Leader: Hear the violent urgings of the marauders.

(Pause.)

> [8]O daughter Babylon, you devastator!
> Happy shall they be who pay you back
> what you have done to us!
> [9]Happy shall they be who take your little ones
> and dash them against the rock!

Leader: Imagine the hatred and anger that have welled up in the psalmist.

(Pause.)

Leader: Now hear the words of Jesus, who said:

You that are accursed, depart from me into the eternal fire prepared for the devil and his angels. (Mt 25:41)

Not everyone . . . will enter the kingdom of heaven, but only the one who does the will of my Father in heaven. On that day many will say to me. "Lord, Lord, did we not prophesy in your name, and cast out demons in your name, and do many deeds of power in your name?" Then I will declare to them, "I never knew you; go away from me, you evildoers." (Mt 7:21-23)

And hear these words of Jesus, who also said:

You have heard that it was said, "You shall love your neighbor and hate your enemy." But I say to you, Love your enemies and pray for those who persecute you, so that you may be children of your Father in heaven. . . . Be perfect, therefore, as your heavenly Father is perfect. (Mt 5:43-45, 48)

Lord, Jesus Christ, we hear the psalmist curse his enemies. We hear you tell us not to do so in both the Old and New Testaments. We know, however, that you are righteous and your judgments are just. We leave to you the proper judgment of all humankind. We know that you have borne the sin of humankind, that you were "wounded for our transgressions, crushed for our iniquities," and that "by [your] bruises we are healed" (Is 53:5). We thank and praise you for this!

Surely we know that our response today is not to curse either our enemies or yours but to return good for evil. Lord, only by your power can we fulfill our commitment to live by this light you have shed on our lives. So, Lord, be present with us. Let your perfection shine through our lives! Amen.

Some Parting Words

Oddly enough, because Psalm 137 is so historically specific, there are many ways to pray it. The directed prayer is relatively generic, but if there is a specific current injustice that cries out for vengeance, when Psalm 137 is placed in the context of the cross of Christ and his commands to us, it can serve as a model for our response.

The God Who Knows Me
Psalm 139

T he crown of all the psalms," says one reader. "This psalm contains for modern man more valuable material for reflection than a psychological, introspective plumbing of one's motivations," says Stanley Jaki. And the redoubtable Charles Spurgeon, whom you know by now to be one of my favorite reflectors on the Psalms, waxes eloquent: "The brightness of this Psalm is like unto a sapphire stone, or Ezekiel's 'terrible crystal'; it flames out with such flashes of light as to turn night into day."

For us it will begin as a respite from the awe-full Psalm 137 and a return to the comfort afforded by Psalm 84. How it concludes will depend on the spiritual condition of each of us as readers. So let us get to our task.

INITIAL READING OF PSALM 139

Psalm 139
To the leader. Of David. A Psalm.

> ¹O LORD, you have searched me and known me.
> ²You know when I sit down and when I rise up;
>   you discern my thoughts from far away.
> ³You search out my path and my lying down,

and are acquainted with all my ways.
⁴Even before a word is on my tongue,
    O LORD, you know it completely.
⁵You hem me in, behind and before,
    and lay your hand upon me.
⁶Such knowledge is too wonderful for me;
    it is so high that I cannot attain it.

⁷Where can I go from your spirit?
    Or where can I flee from your presence?
⁸If I ascend to heaven, you are there;
    if I make my bed in Sheol, you are there.
⁹If I take the wings of the morning
    and settle at the farthest limits of the sea,
¹⁰even there your hand shall lead me,
    and your right hand shall hold me fast.
¹¹If I say, "Surely the darkness shall cover me;
    and the light around me become night,"
¹²even the darkness is not dark to you;
    the night is as bright as the day,
    for darkness is as light to you.

¹³For it was you who formed my inward parts;
    you knit me together in my mother's womb.
¹⁴I praise you, for I am fearfully and wonderfully made.
    Wonderful are your works;
that I know very well.
¹⁵   My frame was not hidden from you,
when I was being made in secret,
    intricately woven in the depths of the earth.

[16]Your eyes beheld my unformed substance.

In your book were written

all the days that were formed for me,

when none of them as yet existed.

[17]How weighty to me are your thoughts, O God!

How vast is the sum of them!

[18]I try to count them—they are more than the sand;

I come to the end—I am still with you.

[19]O that you would kill the wicked, O God,

and that the bloodthirsty would depart from me—

[20]those who speak of you maliciously,

and lift themselves up against you for evil!

[21]Do I not hate those who hate you, O LORD?

And do I not loathe those who rise up against you?

[22]I hate them with perfect hatred;

I count them my enemies.

[23]Search me, O God, and know my heart;

test me and know my thoughts.

[24]See if there is any wicked way in me,

and lead me in the way everlasting.

Be sure before you continue here that you spend considerable time reading and rereading the psalm. By now you surely know why. Forgive me for continuing to say this, but it is important enough to risk your irritation!

GETTING AT THE MEANING OF PSALM 139

You will have realized by now that this psalm poses few problems. Scholars and translators have, of course, found some matters to be difficult, but most of them are solved by the translators (though in slightly different ways), and we need not be troubled by them. So we turn to our usual first concern: to be sure we see the flow of concepts.

Rational Structure

God knows me inside and out: the omniscience of God

    ¹O LORD, you have searched me and known me.

    ²You know when I sit down and when I rise up;

        you discern my thoughts from far away.

    ³You search out my path and my lying down,

        and are acquainted with all my ways.

    ⁴Even before a word is on my tongue,

        O LORD, you know it completely.

    ⁵You hem me in, behind and before,

        and lay your hand upon me.

    ⁶Such knowledge is too wonderful for me;

        it is so high that I cannot attain it.

God is inescapable: the omnipresence of God

    ⁷Where can I go from your spirit?

        Or where can I flee from your presence?

    ⁸If I ascend to heaven, you are there;

        if I make my bed in Sheol, you are there.

    ⁹If I take the wings of the morning

        and settle at the farthest limits of the sea,

    ¹⁰even there your hand shall lead me,

        and your right hand shall hold me fast.

    ¹¹If I say, "Surely the darkness shall cover me;

and the light around me become night,"
[12]even the darkness is not dark to you;

the night is as bright as the day,

for darkness is as light to you.

God is my intimate Creator: the omnipotence of God

[13]For it was you who formed my inward parts;

you knit me together in my mother's womb.

[14]I praise you, for I am fearfully and wonderfully made.

Wonderful are your works;

that I know very well.

[15]   My frame was not hidden from you,

when I was being made in secret,

intricately woven in the depths of the earth.

[16]Your eyes beheld my unformed substance.

In your book were written

all the days that were formed for me,

when none of them as yet existed.

[17]How weighty to me are your thoughts, O God!

How vast is the sum of them!

[18]I try to count them—they are more than the sand;

I come to the end—I am still with you.

Prayer for God to punish the wicked: God is a righteous Judge

[19]O that you would kill the wicked, O God,

and that the bloodthirsty would depart from me—

[20]those who speak of you maliciously,

and lift themselves up against you for evil!

[21]Do I not hate those who hate you, O LORD?

And do I not loathe those who rise up against you?
²²I hate them with perfect hatred;

I count them my enemies.

Prayer for personal righteousness

²³Search me, O God, and know my heart;

test me and know my thoughts.
²⁴See if there is any wicked way in me,

and lead me in the way everlasting.

The structure of Psalm 139 is straightforward. There are four main sections. Each of the first three advances the argument by adding more and more content to the general proposition that God is the greatest—all knowing, everywhere present and all powerful, in that order.

There are two aspects to the powerful impact the psalm makes on us. One is to notice that everything about God is cast in personal terms. God is not just omniscient: he knows *me*. The intimate language and the thought it conveys makes the psalm rich in emotional depth. At the same time, the theological and philosophical points are so strongly asserted that theologians and Christian philosophers constantly turn to Psalm 139 to document their case for the nature of God as omniscient, omnipresent and omnipotent. Truly this theological poem is a stern rejoinder both to scholars who treat biblical texts as footnotes to their own painstakingly framed systematic theology and pastors who ignore the profundity of the ideas and turn the psalm into psychological therapy. God is not God without being a caring Person characterized by infinite and absolute intelligence, power, presence and righteousness.

In the first section (vv. 1-6), the psalmist marvels over the fact that God knows everything about him—his actions (sitting and rising), his thoughts and his words before he speaks them. He is in awe of God's very personal and intimate knowledge of him. Notice especially that this knowledge does not cause in him any sense of guilt. He is pleased that God knows him so well.

I want to say, "Isn't this amazing?" Do you? When you know God knows you from stem to stern, can you be so pleased? Some commentators have thought this indicates the psalmist's naiveté or arrogance. Are not we sinners deserving of God's wrath? Are not confession and repentance required before we can be so confident that God will not weigh us and find us wanting? Regardless, the psalmist is so given to his love for God and God's righteousness that such thoughts are not present here.

In the second section (vv. 7-12), the psalmist ponders the inescapable God. He is everywhere, in the heights of heaven and the shadowland of the dead, and everywhere he is the psalmist's personal guide and protector—day and night utterly aware and in control.

The third section (vv. 13-18) contemplates God as Creator of the psalmist's every last atom of every last inner part, from conception to delivery through every moment of every day. God works wonders, one of which is the psalmist! God's wisdom and thoughts are vaster than the universe.

Throughout the psalm, we see the psalmist straining after language that will express the awe and wonder he contemplates—*wings of the morning, farthest limits of the sea, darkness is as light, intricately woven, weighty thoughts.* Each takes its place in the gathering intricacy of the vision of God's knowing and powerful Presence.

The fourth section (vv. 19-24) makes an abrupt shift in both content and emotion: from worshipful awe to righteous indignation. During your readings of the psalm, were you struck by this change? When I finally paid proper attention to the psalm, I was, and sometimes am all over again. This is not unusual. "Many Christian readers feel that this sudden prayer sounds a jarring note after what has gone before," says John Stott. "Yet it is perfectly consistent with it. When a man's world is full of God, he longs for the elimination of evil." I think Stott has taken the right tack here. These lines are not hate filled and "thrown in," as C. S. Lewis judges, "almost childishly." They arise out of the reflections of a man who sees himself as siding with God. He is calling for vengeance not against his own enemies but against God's enemies. This theme of imprecation was treated in the previous chapter (pp. 154-67), and I will not repeat that discussion.

There is, however, another explanation for the cursing of the wicked. Some scholars think that this psalm did not so much arise out of the psalmist's independent meditation of the character of God but rather from a situation in which he had been unjustly accused of idolatry. The whole psalm is then seen as a plea to God to judge the psalmist by God's own infinite and intimate knowledge. This makes the fourth section the logical culmination of a case vindicating the psalmist's character. I am not convinced, however, that this is the correct setting for the psalm and generally follow the readings of John Stott, Charles Spurgeon and Derek Kidner who make no mention of this interpretation.

The key to this psalm comes, so it seems to me, in the final two verses (vv. 23-24), when the psalmist calls on God to *search* him and *know* him, to *test* him and *know* his thoughts. This would be sheer audacity if the psalmist were not confident that God would see him as one of his own. What makes this psalm so valuable for answering speech is that one of the great poets/psalmists of the ancient world felt free to boldly come before the throne of God. It was by faith that Abraham offered up Isaac. It was by faith that all the great saints of the Hebrew Scriptures lived and moved and had their being (Heb 11). So it is here. It is by faith that the psalmist can come before God and delight in the knowledge that God knows him profoundly, will never depart from him and will do all that was necessary for him to live *in the way everlasting.*

We can come boldly before the throne for the same reason as the psalmist. God is good enough, compassionate enough and great enough to accept us as one of his forever family. We know the role Jesus Christ played in making this possible. The psalmist did not. But the psalmist had everything we too need—utter confidence in the great, righteous, omniscient, omnipresent, omnipotent God himself. His prayer can be our answering speech.

PRAYING PSALM 139

Read through the psalm again, reacquainting yourself with its felt thought. Then make it your answering speech.

> ¹O LORD, you have searched me and known me.
> ²You know when I sit down and when I rise up;
>> you discern my thoughts from far away.
> ³You search out my path and my lying down,
>> and are acquainted with all my ways.

Respond: *Lord, I want to make these lines and those that follow my own lines. Let me enter into them. Let me absorb their meaning and turn them back to you as my own.* Pause. Then repeat as prayer verses 1-3. Pause and then continue with the psalm.

> ⁴Even before a word is on my tongue,
>> O LORD, you know it completely.

Respond: *Do you really know what I am going to say? Of course you do. May I be more conscious of this so that all my speech honors you.*

⁵You hem me in, behind and before,
>   and lay your hand upon me.

Respond: *Lord, you surround me with your presence. I am indeed at all times in the Presence. I live and move and have my being in you. And yet you honor me with individuality. You do not absorb me into yourself so that there is no "me" left. You lay your hand on me!*

⁶Such knowledge is too wonderful for me;
>   it is so high that I cannot attain it.

Respond: *Too high! Too high! Too wonderful! Too wonderful!*
Pause.
Respond again: *Too high! Too high! Too wonderful! Too wonderful!*

⁷Where can I go from your spirit?
>   Or where can I flee from your presence?
⁸If I ascend to heaven, you are there;
>   if I make my bed in Sheol, you are there.
⁹If I take the wings of the morning
>   and settle at the farthest limits of the sea,
¹⁰even there your hand shall lead me,
>   and your right hand shall hold me fast.

Respond: *O Lord, this is wonderful too! Your presence means you are always with me, always there to receive my arrow prayers. In the midst of business, in the midst of leisure, in the midst of my family, you are there.* Survey where you have been in the past twenty-four hours, the past week, the past month, the past year, and tell God you know he has been with you. If there are special times of either success or failure when you especially sensed his presence, recount those.

¹¹If I say, "Surely the darkness shall cover me;

and the light around me become night,"
¹²even the darkness is not dark to you;
>   the night is as bright as the day,
>   for darkness is as light to you.

Respond: *O Lord, in the darkness of night, you know my thoughts.* You may feel obliged to confess that here some of them have not been right. *You know my deeds.* Again confession may be in order. Yet since this is not a penitential psalm, you needn't turn it into one. Move on quickly to the next verses.

¹³For it was you who formed my inward parts;
>   you knit me together in my mother's womb.
¹⁴I praise you, for I am fearfully and wonderfully made.
>   Wonderful are your works;
>   that I know very well.
¹⁵   My frame was not hidden from you,
>   when I was being made in secret,
>   intricately woven in the depths of the earth.
¹⁶Your eyes beheld my unformed substance.

Respond: Imagine this scene. *Thank you, Lord, for your presence even as I was a baby in my mother's womb. Thank you for a successful delivery. Thank you for my life itself. Wonderful are your works!*

In your book were written
>   all the days that were formed for me,
>   when none of them as yet existed.

Respond: *I never know just how to understand your great foreknowledge of all events down to the movements of the last atom. And I certainly don't understand your foreknowledge of me. I am glad I do not have such knowledge. It wasn't meant for your children.*

¹⁷How weighty to me are your thoughts, O God!

How vast is the sum of them!

¹⁸I try to count them—they are more than the sand;

I come to the end—I am still with you.

Respond: *Indeed, Lord, I can't even begin to fathom your thoughts. Let me just pause and wait. I know I will never come to the end of your mind. Behold, I am, and still will be, with you.*

Pause.

¹⁹O that you would kill the wicked, O God,

and that the bloodthirsty would depart from me—

²⁰those who speak of you maliciously,

and lift themselves up against you for evil!

²¹Do I not hate those who hate you, O LORD?

And do I not loathe those who rise up against you?

²²I hate them with perfect hatred;

I count them my enemies.

Respond: *I am shocked by the psalmist here. Suddenly amid the glorious vision of you as all knowing and all powerful and everywhere present, the psalmist is reminded of your entire righteousness and yearns for the deliverance of your kingdom from the presence of evil. Teach me what it is to hate with a perfect hatred. But in the meantime, help me to be righteous.*

²³Search me, O God, and know my heart;

test me and know my thoughts.

²⁴See if there is any wicked way in me,

and lead me in the way everlasting.

Respond: *Lord, let me pause while I concentrate on the impact on me of praying this prayer.*

Pause.

Respond: Repeat as a prayer the final words (vv. 23-24). *Amen.*

SOME FURTHER REFLECTIONS

Psalm 139 is loaded with theology. Why not reflect on specifically theological themes of omniscience, omnipresence, omnipotence and righteousness? Put the text of the psalm on one or two sheets, and highlight in different colors the phrases and images that relate to each of these terms. What do you see? A rational pattern? An aesthetic "logic"? An emotional dimension? Then repray the psalm from what you now see and seem to understand—or not understand!

All of the psalms can be examined in this fashion. There is nothing magical about the method; it just helps to concentrate the mind and focus the emotions. The Holy Spirit is the One finally in control.

Small Group Study of Psalm 139

The following comments are directed to the leader.

Introduction

This psalm focuses on the experience of one person. You should not try to make it corporate, but let each participant take his or her own thought path as you study and pray it.

Group Instruction and Questions

1. Have one person read Psalm 139 in its entirety at an ordinary pace.

2. Have another person read it very slowly, with a pause after each verse.

3. Continue with a third reading.

4. What strikes you about this psalm? (This general question is designed to get out first impressions. To such a question there are no wrong answers. But if in the discussion of later questions something really off base doesn't get corrected, you may wish to return to the issue and clarify the earlier "misimpression.")

5. Have someone put titles to each of the four sections of the psalm.

   What is the general flow of the ideas? (You may need to suggest the relevance of the theological terms—*omniscience, omnipresence, omnipotence* and *righteousness*—to the various sections.)

6. What does God know about us?

   How conscious of this are we? Why?

7. Why is God inescapable?

   Does the psalmist want to escape?

Do you? Why?

8. A dramatic shift of topic and emphasis occurs between verses 18 and 19. Why do you think the psalmist shifts focus so radically?

9. What shift in emotion occurs at the same place?

   How does that tie in with the shift of topic?

10. How does what we studied about imprecation (regarding Psalm 137) relate to our overall understanding of this psalm?

11. How do the final two verses form a fitting conclusion to the psalm?

12. How does our position in Christ affect what we mean by praying these verses?

   When you believe the group is ready to make Psalm 139 its prayer, proceed as directed.

DIRECTED PRAYER

Leader: Let us pray through Psalm 139. We will start by praying aloud together the first three verses:

¹O LORD, you have searched me and known me.
²You know when I sit down and when I rise up;
     you discern my thoughts from far away.
³You search out my path and my lying down,
     and are acquainted with all my ways.

Leader: Try to realize God's profound knowledge of you.
   (Pause. Then read the next verse.)

⁴Even before a word is on my tongue,
     O LORD, you know it completely.

Leader: Reflect on what God knows about your thoughts and attitudes and how they influence your own words. The good words and appropriate ones, the ones you later come to regret. Yield your words to the lordship of Christ.

(Pause.)

> [5]You hem me in, behind and before,
>   and lay your hand upon me.

Leader: Envision the invisible God with his arm on your shoulder. Is he even now suggesting a path to take?

(Pause.)

> [6]Such knowledge is too wonderful for me;
>   it is so high that I cannot attain it.

Leader: Wait before the Lord.

(Pause.)

> [7]Where can I go from your spirit?
>   Or where can I flee from your presence?
> [8]If I ascend to heaven, you are there;
>   if I make my bed in Sheol, you are there.
> [9]If I take the wings of the morning
>   and settle at the farthest limits of the sea,
> [10]even there your hand shall lead me,
>   and your right hand shall hold me fast.
> [11]If I say, "Surely the darkness shall cover me;
>   and the light around me become night,"
> [12]even the darkness is not dark to you;
>   the night is as bright as the day,
>   for darkness is as light to you.

Leader: Think about any attempts you have made to avoid God. Did they work? What do you learn from this? Thank God for teaching you.

(Pause.)

Leader: Recall any special times you have felt or "known" God's presence. Thank him for always being there, even when you are not aware of him.

(Pause.)

> [13]For it was you who formed my inward parts;
>> you knit me together in my mother's womb.
> [14]I praise you, for I am fearfully and wonderfully made.
>> Wonderful are your works;
> that I know very well.
> [15]   My frame was not hidden from you,
> when I was being made in secret,
>> intricately woven in the depths of the earth.
> [16]Your eyes beheld my unformed substance.

Leader: As I slowly reread these lines, call up mental images of them. (Reread the lines, pausing after each image. Then pause a little longer at the end of verse 16.)

> In your book were written
>> all the days that were formed for me,
>> when none of them as yet existed.

Leader: Thank God for his exhaustive knowledge of you—beginning to end.

(Pause.)

> [17]How weighty to me are your thoughts, O God!
>> How vast is the sum of them!

¹⁸I try to count them—they are more than the sand;
>   I come to the end—I am still with you.

Leader: Imagine counting from one to infinity. Will you ever come to the end?

(Pause.)

¹⁹O that you would kill the wicked, O God,
>   and that the bloodthirsty would depart from me—
²⁰those who speak of you maliciously,
>   and lift themselves up against you for evil!
²¹Do I not hate those who hate you, O LORD?
>   And do I not loathe those who rise up against you?
²²I hate them with perfect hatred;
>   I count them my enemies.

Leader: You may not feel the same indignation at evil as the psalmist does. But recall some of the public expressions of evil you are aware of, such as terrorism, corporate fraud, child abusers . . . Now side with the psalmist and call on God to right wrongs and bring justice to bear on the oppressors and relief to the oppressed. Be specific.

(Pause.)

Leader: We turn now to look at our own relationship with God as the righteous One who is present with us. (Read the final two verses.)

²³Search me, O God, and know my heart;
>   test me and know my thoughts.
²⁴See if there is any wicked way in me,
>   and lead me in the way everlasting.

Leader: Now let us repeat together the final two verses. (Read together verses 23-24.) Amen.

SOME PARTING REMARKS

This is a rather emotional psalm. Some in the group may want to talk with others about what they experienced as they prayed it.

Our Mighty Fortress
Psalm 46

Ιt is Sunday afternoon on a ranch in Nebraska. My family has not attended church; we live too far from any town to do that. Electrical lines are not yet strung as far into the plains as our house, but we have a small battery radio. From its tiny speaker come the strains of a beautiful hymn. *The Lutheran Hour* is on the air and "A Mighty Fortress Is Our God" is sounding forth.

This early childhood memory is rich in nostalgia. I never want to live that way again, but I wouldn't change the experience for having grown up anywhere else. I had no idea then that Martin Luther's hymn was really inspired by an ancient Hebrew psalm. Now that psalm is one of my favorites. Psalm 46 is pointed, positive and powerful. It will make an appropriate climax to this set of psalms.

INITIAL READING OF PSALM 46

Psalm 46

To the leader. Of the Korahites. According to Alamoth. A Song.

> [1]God is our refuge and strength,
> > a very present help in trouble.

²Therefore we will not fear, though the earth should change,
> though the mountains shake in the heart of the sea;

³though its waters roar and foam,
> though the mountains tremble with its tumult. *Selah*

⁴There is a river whose streams make glad the city of God,
> the holy habitation of the Most High.

⁵God is in the midst of the city; it shall not be moved;
> God will help it when the morning dawns.

⁶The nations are in an uproar, the kingdoms totter;
> he utters his voice, the earth melts.

⁷The LORD of hosts is with us;
> the God of Jacob is our refuge. *Selah*

⁸Come, behold the works of the LORD;
> see what desolations he has brought on the earth.

⁹He makes wars cease to the end of the earth;
> he breaks the bow, and shatters the spear;
> he burns the shields with fire.

¹⁰"Be still, and know that I am God!
> I am exalted among the nations,
> I am exalted in the earth."

¹¹The LORD of hosts is with us;
> the God of Jacob is our refuge. *Selah*

Reread this psalm until you have both felt and understood the flow of ideas and can participate in its language.

GETTING AT THE MEANING OF PSALM 46

This psalm of praise is carefully crafted, a joy to analyze as well as pray.

Rational Structure

The flow of ideas is again straightforward and easy to follow.

God is our refuge: Invocation

¹God is our refuge and strength,
a very present help in trouble.

God is sovereign over nature

²Therefore we will not fear, though the earth should change,
though the mountains shake in the heart of the sea;
³though its waters roar and foam,
though the mountains tremble with its tumult. *Selah*

⁴There is a river whose streams make glad the city of God,
the holy habitation of the Most High.
⁵God is in the midst of the city; it shall not be moved;
God will help it when the morning dawns.

God is sovereign over the nations

⁶The nations are in an uproar, the kingdoms totter;
he utters his voice, the earth melts.
⁷The LORD of hosts is with us;
the God of Jacob is our refuge.   *Selah*

God is sovereign over the future

⁸Come, behold the works of the LORD;
see what desolations he has brought on the earth.
⁹He makes wars cease to the end of the earth;
he breaks the bow, and shatters the spear;
he burns the shields with fire.

"Listen! I am in control!"

[10]"Be still, and know that I am God!
    I am exalted among the nations,
    I am exalted in the earth."

God is our refuge: Benediction

[11]The LORD of hosts is with us;
    the God of Jacob is our refuge.   *Selah*

This psalm contains one of the most well-known phrases in the Old Testament. The number of sermons that have been preached on it must number as the sands of the sea. And many of them, orthodox as they may have been in terms of content, have twisted the Scripture to fit an idea the psalm was never intended to promote.

This is a bold assertion. Let's see if I can substantiate it. I have often begun a lecture entitled "Scripture Twisting" by asking the audience, "What does this Bible verse mean: 'Be still, and know that I am God'?" The responses inevitably include statements like these: "Meditate and you will experience the presence of God," or "Stop thinking. Turn off your mind. God will reveal himself to you." Now, given the proper circumstances and preparation, this may well be the case. Biblical meditation is indeed a spiritual discipline, as we have already seen in Psalm 130. The problem is that Psalm 46:10 is not about meditation. What then does it mean? The answer is in the context.

The entire psalm is a unified paean of praise to God as utterly in control over all possible circumstances. It ends as it begins, proclaiming God as our refuge and strength. God is sovereign over nature and nations, both now and in the future. In the midst of praising God for his protection, come what may, the psalmist issues God's command. God's command to the psalmist and to the reader simply means "Be still" or "Shut up" or

"Listen up!" or "Stop flailing around, worrying about the outcome. I am in charge." As a command to violent nature and violent nations it means, "Hold it, earth! You will not mess up my world. Stop it, armies and terrorists! You will not exterminate my people!" These parallel Jesus' command to the turbulent Lake of Galilee: "Peace! Be still" (Mk 4: 39). Verse 10 has nothing to do with meditation.

Verse 10 does, however, have an important application. It means that whenever we are beset by potential danger or actual disaster, we can know that God not only knows about this but is in charge of the entire situation. We can—we should—cease striving to solve our problems on our own and realize that God is with us in the midst of them. His will will be done.

Emotional Structure

As is often the case, the rhetorical power of this psalm comes from the vivid imagery. The phrases *mountains shake in the heart of the sea* and *the earth melts* bring to my mind the great Hawaiian mountains rising out of the middle of the Pacific Ocean. Mauna Kea is the largest mountain in the world; beginning 18,000 feet under the sea, it peaks at 13,796 feet. Mauna Kea is inactive now, but thirty miles away the Kilauea volcano still pours lava into the ocean, and needles on seismographs at Volcano National Park on the "Big Island" jiggle away, vividly showing that all of Hawaii is constantly in motion. Down at the sea ten miles away *the waters roar and foam.* Today Kilauea is a great tourist attraction, but residents of the island who have lost their homes to red-hot flowing lava know that danger lurks behind every jiggle of the needle. Yet God is in charge.

Nations are in an uproar and *kingdoms totter.* The ancient Hebrews may not have known the terror of atomic weapons or envisioned the devastation of Hiroshima. They may not have imagined two planes crashing into tall towers in faraway future New York. But they experienced sieges of their own cities and the carnage of their own battles. They saw kings and kingdoms rise and fall. Yet God was in charge.

They may have known about *a river whose streams make glad the city of God*— Zion. The image is of peace and security established and maintained by the Most High. There they knew that God was in charge. But they knew that they might see it only *when the morning dawns.*

They had not yet experienced the end of wars, neither local nor worldwide. They had not seen what the psalmist did—*God breaks the bow, and shatters the spear* and *burns the shields with fire.* The psalmist here turns apocalyptic prophet. When the world's history wraps up, when in the fullness of time God's kingdom comes, wars will *cease to the end of the earth.*

Psalm 46, then, is both a reminder of God's presence with them and a prophecy of his continued care. It is a product of hope, not hope based solely on blind faith but predicated on their understanding of who God really was and is and will continue to be. Their faith can become ours as we make Psalm 46 our answering speech. God is our refuge and strength— a very present help in time of trouble!

PRAYING PSALM 146

Read through the entire psalm again. Then with eyes open, read and pray section by section. This is a corporate psalm. You are now alone with God. So as you pray it, realize that you are praying as one of your community of faith, one of God's forever family made up of millions of people past, present and future.

> [1]God is our refuge and strength,
> > a very present help in trouble.

Respond: *Lord, you are my refuge and strength, and not mine alone. You are the refuge and strength of all those in all times and all places who put their trust in you. You are the One, you are the only, you are the one and only magnificent and great God!*

²Therefore we will not fear, though the earth should change,
       though the mountains shake in the heart of the sea;
³though its waters roar and foam,
       though the mountains tremble with its tumult. *Selah*

Respond: *Lord, I see the logic. I see the* therefore *and I see* why *it is there. Of course I will not fear—at least when I remember in the depth of my heart why I need not fear. I have seen, or at least know about, some of the wonders the psalmist pictures, the shaking of the seismograph needle, the lava spurting out like tea from a teapot into the boiling ocean. I have seen the hot bubbling of the waters of Yellowstone and know about the molten core of earth.* You have created them. *Recall some of your own experiences with nature's power. They are yours. If you have them in control, you have all of the earth under your care. Therefore I will not fear in any of my circumstances.* Name some of your own troubles. *You are in control of all the problems my community faces.* Name some of them. *You are in control of the troubles of Christians everywhere.* Name some of those you know. *I speak as best I can for all my friends: We will not fear though the mountains fall into the sea.*

⁴There is a river whose streams make glad the city of God,
       the holy habitation of the Most High.
⁵God is in the midst of the city; it shall not be moved;
       God will help it when the morning dawns.

Respond: *I see that city set on a hill. I see a pleasant stream. I see the temple in Zion. True, it's only my imagination, but it helps me see you as resident with the ancient Hebrews. And I know your habitation now is in the hearts of your children. When I contemplate your presence, I see that there is a stream in my own heart too and a stream that flows by my community of faith. It gladdens my heart. It gladdens my congregation. I know that this pleasant scene may not be a present reality, but it will be when the morning dawns. It will be when the Lord returns and his kingdom comes.*

⁶The nations are in an uproar, the kingdoms totter;
he utters his voice, the earth melts.

Respond: *So much violence from so much terror! So many bombs and suicide bombers! So many places where genocide is the order of the day! Are you really in charge? Yes, I know it. But I don't see it. Lord, that you would speak! That your voice would melt the earth and stem the violence! I cry out for your judgment on us as your people. But I cry out only in hope.*

⁷The LORD of hosts is with us;
the God of Jacob is our refuge.   *Selah*

Respond: *Yes, Lord of hosts, you are with us! Oh be our refuge!*

⁸Come, behold the works of the LORD;
see what desolations he has brought on the earth.
⁹He makes wars cease to the end of the earth;
he breaks the bow, and shatters the spear;
he burns the shields with fire.

Respond: *I hear the psalmist predict the end of wars as if they were already over. I see his vision like that of Isaiah. He has seen in his mind's eye what you have put there as prophecy. I now see it too. Peace on earth, good will among people! Make this vision my goal for this earth. Make me a person of peace.*

¹⁰"Be still, and know that I am God!
I am exalted among the nations,
I am exalted in the earth."

Respond: *Now I hear your voice. May it break through my consciousness into my heart!*

May you transform me so that I see beyond the shaking earth, beyond the feuding nations. Pause. Be still. Wait on the Lord. Let verse 10 sink deeper into your being. Then repeat it as a prayer.

> [11]The LORD of hosts is with us;
>> the God of Jacob is our refuge.   *Selah*

Respond: *You are with us, Lord, with my community, my friends serving you in other parts of your world. You are our refuge and strength! Amen.*

SOME FURTHER THOUGHTS

Did you notice the irony of the prayer liturgy just presented? I had said that verse 10 is not about meditation. But when we got to verse 10, the instruction was to "Pause. Be still. Wait on the Lord." Why? Because that is the way to absorb the central message of the psalm. The message is not that if we meditate we will experience God. The message is that God is in charge of all reality, that what he wills happens and we should stop trying to take his job on ourselves. But the way to get that message is to *be still* in another way—that is, to meditate.

In the final analysis, though, this psalm requires of us what we cannot fully give. Our confidence in God wavers. We are not at ease in this troubled world. We do not see, except in times of deep meditation, the end of wars and the glories of the peaceful kingdom. There is never a time in our spiritual life when we shouldn't turn to this psalm. As our answering speech, it will help us move closer and closer to a God's-eye view of both the past and the present and, even more important, a God's-eye view of the future.

Small Group Study of Psalm 46

The following comments are directed to the leader.

Introduction

This psalm may well have been used in ancient Hebrew public worship and is easily applicable to group use today.

Group Instruction and Questions

1. Have one person read Psalm 46 in its entirety at an ordinary pace.

2. Have another person read it very slowly, with a pause after each verse.

3. A third reading is certainly appropriate.

4. What phrase or phrases stuck out as we slowly read the psalm? (Some may mention the poetic phrases, but surely some one or more people will mention verse 10. So follow that up with the next question.)

5. What do you think is meant by verse 10? (Take several answers. Someone will probably mention meditation to "know" God. Have the group continue to answer the question till someone notices that the verse doesn't mean that and explains why. It is always best for participants to correct themselves rather than for you to correct them. Still, in the end you may have to do so.)

6. What is the central idea of the psalm? How many times is it repeated?

   What does it mean for God to be a *refuge* and *strength?*

7. What is the flow of ideas?

   Have someone (or more) title the sections of the psalm (see pp. 198-99).

8. Give some recent examples of manifestations of nature's power.

9. Give some modern examples of *nations . . . in an uproar.*

10. Has the psalmist's vision of the future been fulfilled?

   Do you see any indication that it will take place?

   Why, then, is the psalmist so certain? (Be sure you discuss the notion of *hope*, not as logical calculation, nor as pipe dream, but as resting in the character of God.)

11. How is God a refuge and strength to you and your (our) community?

   When you think the group is ready to make Psalm 46 their prayer, lead them as follows.

DIRECTED PRAYER

Use the following script to lead the group in prayer.

Leader: Let us pray together the first verse:

   ¹God is our refuge and strength,
      a very present help in trouble.

   (Pause.)

   ²Therefore we will not fear, though the earth should change,
      though the mountains shake in the heart of the sea;
   ³though its waters roar and foam,
      though the mountains tremble with its tumult. *Selah*

Leader: Imagine standing at the foot of an erupting volcano whose lava is flowing into a boiling sea. Are you afraid? Remember that God is your refuge and strength. Do you fear now? Tell God what you feel and how much you crave his presence as refuge and strength.

(Pause.)
> [4]There is a river whose streams make glad the city of God,
>> the holy habitation of the Most High.
> [5]God is in the midst of the city; it shall not be moved;
>> God will help it when the morning dawns.

Leader: Now imagine the city of God, high on a hill overlooking a verdant valley and a quiet but powerful river. Think of God's presence here, securing the city from harm. Imagine this peaceful city surrounded by raging violence outside the walls, terror that will cease only *when morning comes.*

(Pause.)

> [6]The nations are in an uproar, the kingdoms totter;
>> he utters his voice, the earth melts.

Leader: Now turn your attention to the nations that are surrounding the city and preparing a siege. See them move their armies into place. And then see confusion set in and the very earth melt as their forces retreat.

(Pause.)

> [7]The LORD of hosts is with us;
>> the God of Jacob is our refuge.   *Selah*

Leader: Let us say this verse together. (Repeat verse 7.)

> [8]Come, behold the works of the LORD;
>> see what desolations he has brought on the earth.
> [9]He makes wars cease to the end of the earth;
>> he breaks the bow, and shatters the spear;

Leader: Imagine this scene. Make it modern. Imagine the destruction of our weapons and the weapons of all who oppose us.

(Pause.)

Leader: Now hear the voice of God that the psalmist heard.

> [10]"Be still, and know that I am God!
>   I am exalted among the nations,
>   I am exalted in the earth."

Leader: Let us be still and know that God is our refuge and strength.

(Pause. This should be a longer pause than most. When you think it appropriate, continue.)

Leader: Let's pray together the final verse of the psalm.

> [11]The LORD of hosts is with us;
>   the God of Jacob is our refuge.   *Selah*

Leader: And all God's children said, [pause and say together], Amen!

A fitting way to end the group prayer is by singing "A Mighty Fortress Is Our God."

SOME PARTING REMARKS

John Stott says that Martin Luther and Philipp Melanchthon together used to sing "Ein' feste Burg ist unser Gott" (i.e., "A Mighty Fortress Is Our God") "in times of dark discouragement." So too, as leader, you might recommend both that and a return to Psalm 46 for a rejuvenation of confidence in God's control even when everything around is falling apart. It is likewise notable that John Wesley died shortly after paraphrasing the last line of the psalm: "The best of all is, God is with us."

ELEVEN

Teach Us to Pray

In some ways this book has been an easy one for me to write. I did not need to spend hours and hours in the library, chasing down articles in learned journals or poring over crumbling ancient manuscripts to ferret out esoteric knowledge long lost to the modern world. Everything was there in front of me: several translations of the Bible with the text of the Psalms, a few basic commentaries by some reputable scholars, and a lifetime of sometimes casual, sometimes intense reading and praying of the psalms. The topic is dear to my heart. I am delighted to be able to address it and share with others what I have learned.

But in one major way this book has been difficult. The problem is the topic itself—not the psalms, the texts and their meaning, but prayer. The essence of this book is neither academic nor primarily intellectual, as many of my other books have been. The essence of this book is deeply *spiritual.* It pretends to be a guide to a deeper, more intimate life more and more finely tuned to the reality of God. That has put on me an extra burden. I must not just be as correct as possible about what any given psalm might mean; more important, I must not mislead readers in their spiritual lives.

Blaise Pascal hid in the lining of his jacket a record of his own deep spiritual experience of God's presence as "fire" and its aftermath. This record was never intended to be seen by anyone but God himself, nor reflected on by anyone but Pascal himself. How do the great writers on the spiritual life do it? Some do it by what appears to be great candor before their readers. Others do it by focusing their writing almost exclusively on God or Scripture or the insights of others, while talking little about their own experience. In any case, I wonder if they sense the same inadequacy as I do when it comes to giving spiritual direction.

In this book I have combined the two ways, placing, I hope, the emphasis on the second way. What wisdom there is in this book is the wisdom of the psalms and psalmists themselves. At the beck and call of the Holy Spirit, the psalmists wrote their songs of worship, confession, lament, joy and praise. They and the prophets provided for the Hebrew community the language of spiritual reality. And in the translation and repeated reading and praying of these psalms down through the ages, that spiritual reality has come alive in God's children around the world. It is this spiritual reality I earnestly desire for myself and for the readers of this book.

What, then, have we learned by reading and praying the ten psalms? What can be carried away from this exercise that will improve our prayer life when we are not praying the psalms? I want to isolate and emphasize six principles. All of them have been illustrated in the psalms we have prayed. So this will be—wisely, I trust—the shortest chapter in the book.

WE LEARN TO PRAY BY PRAYING

First, praying is not having a theology of prayer; it is not believing that prayer is important; it is not an item in the Sunday morning church program. It is a discipline—an intentionally directed activity. Learning to pray is not like learning sociology; it's like riding a bike.

That has been the premise of this entire book. Now I urge that it become a premise in the further development of our spiritual lives. Prayer is a spiritual discipline. It works only by being worked.

So do it. The more you pray, the more you learn about prayer. The more you learn about prayer by praying, the more you pray. Sure, read books on prayer. They are legion and they can really help. But as the Nike ad says, "Just Do It."

THE GOD TO WHOM WE PRAY

When we pray, we must understand that it is to God that we pray. Today prayer is often touted as self-help for the soul or talking to yourself to solve your self-imposed problems. But the psalms will have none of this. "O Lord" is the address.

"O LORD, you have searched me," begins Psalm 139 and continues with "You . . . You . . . You . . ." over and over. "Answer me when I call, O God of my right!" (Ps 4:1), "Give ear to my words, O LORD" (Ps 5:1), "O LORD my God, in you I take refuge" (Ps 7:1). The psalmist never lets God be far from his mind. Either he is rejoicing in God's power and presence or calling on God to be present when God seems so palpably absent.

The fact of God is foundational. But what is God like? Is he just a cosmic Grand Father? Merely a dynamic force? The psalms teach that he is so much more. In the great personal/theological Psalm 139, God is both personally intimate and theologically absolute in his omnipresence, his omniscience, his omnipotence and his righteousness. He is the One in whom the psalmists all take confidence. He does not always answer their prayers (Ps 42—43), but his character is burned into the psalmist's heart, so that even when God feels absent the psalmist maintains hope, not an airy-fairy empty vision but a robust trust in God's ultimate control (Ps 84). In the end the thirsting deer will be satisfied (Ps 42), the slandered ones will be vindicated (Ps 7). Every psalm carries in its heart a profound underlying conception of the infinite-personal one God, unlike and transcending any other claims to God.

It is the absolute fact of his being the one and only, all-powerful, all-knowing, everywhere-present God that, when combined with his utter, time-out-of-mind righteousness, grounds the absolute rightness of his moral law and his moral judgments. God is not just Being itself ("I AM WHO I AM"). He is *Logos* (Word) and thus intelligence itself. He is also what it is to be Good. In the midst of a broken world, the psalmists often do not always see how he is all these great things. But they never yield (Ps 42—43).

Nor should we. It is such a God to whom we pray. This should cause us to rein in our tendency to see God as the "big guy upstairs" or "my buddy." Our God is an awesome God! Yes, Jesus taught us that God is also "Father," but he is an awesome Father whose light sometimes appears as darkness. He is the God who judges and the One who takes vengeance. "Fear of the Lord" is not an inappropriate attitude. In fact, it is the beginning of wisdom, as one of the psalms we did not pray says (Ps 111:10). In this there is great relief, for it means we do not need to take revenge on either God's enemies or our own. He does so with both justice and mercy.

PRAYER ARISES OUT OF A DISCIPLINED LIFE

The ancient Hebrews, like many religious traditions over the centuries, had regular prescribed times of prayer. Praying three times a day was a longstanding practice that continued into the time of Jesus. As Joachim Jeremias says, "No day in the life of Jesus passed without the three times of prayer: the morning prayer at sunrise, the afternoon prayer at the time when the afternoon sacrifice was offered in the Temple, the evening prayer at night before going to sleep." We have considered two psalms that reflect two of these times (Ps 4 and 5).

The Psalms of Ascent (Ps 120—131) seem to have been set prayers for the pilgrimage to Jerusalem at a festival time. Psalm 137 is a communal lament arising out of reflections on the exile in Babylon. Psalm 84 is another song of Zion, celebrating the city where God makes his presence known.

So, too, today there are formal, established times of prayer in our communities. The psalms, in fact, often are used in our liturgies. This is appropriate. What is not appropriate is the way that these liturgical elements may become so ordinary that their significance almost disappears. In any case, the psalms give us much encouragement to keep prayer in our set liturgical practices.

PRAYER ARISES OUT OF OUR CONDITION

Even more obvious is the fact that the prayer represented by the psalms arises out of our human condition in the world. Out of sin comes confession (Ps 32). Out of the depths of despair arise our laments to God and pleading for his presence (Ps 42—43). Out of the troubles of the day comes an evening prayer (Ps 4). Out of the desire for a day laid in service at the feet of God comes a morning prayer (Ps 5). Out of a situation in which the psalmist has been slandered arises a call to God for proper judgment and vindication (Ps 7). Out of the contemplation of the transcendence and immanence of God arises a psalm of wonderment and awe (Ps 139).

Surely there is no situation in which it is not proper to pray. Better, there is no situation in which prayer should not be a part. Prayer should precede, accompany and follow every moment of our life. May we keep this in mind as we wend our way through the troubles of each day and as we plan for the days ahead. As the apostle Paul says, we should "pray without ceasing," and the psalms give us examples of doing so.

PRAYER RUNS THE GAMUT OF EMOTIONS

How different are the emotional structures of the various psalms! Some begin in agony and end in ecstasy (Ps 5 and 7). Some are launched in joy that only becomes more intense (Ps 84). Others begin in desperation and end only in the hopeful knowledge that one day God will relieve the pain (Ps 42—43). Some rise to a fever pitch of anger and vitriolic hatred (Ps 137). In some anger bursts out unexpectedly (Ps 139). As a whole the psalms follow no emotional rule. Anything goes.

This observation may be one of the more important for our spiritual life. Given the language in the last verse of Psalm 137 and the sustained questioning of Psalms 42—43, what can we not say to God? Are we angry? Spill it out. Are we frustrated? Tell God about it. Let us make our case—whatever it is—before God. He alone is worthy to judge. He alone can take our muttering, sputtering, vitriolic words and make of them something worthy of his kingdom, if by no other means, by transforming our broken spirit, our corrupt will and our erring mind into something beautiful for him.

Honest prayer—is there any other kind?—comes from the depths of our heart. There is no question of fooling God. We cannot sneak up on him with silvery tongue, singing his praises, and at the same time harbor resentment of either him or others. He knows us (Ps 139). How he knows us! Now let us know ourselves by coming close to him. He can do for us what we cannot do for ourselves—heal our broken selves. Confession is good for the soul (Ps 32).

PRAYER TAKES PLACE IN SILENCE

I deliberately placed Psalm 130 as the second of the ten psalms, because after being reminded that God's forgiveness restores us to a right relationship with God (Ps 32), I wanted to introduce the practice of silence. We are a wordy and noisy people. We fill the aural space in our life with talk and music. Our mind trails after the chatter, the melody, the lyrics.

We don't so much listen to what's being said, sung or performed as block out the motions of our own mind and also shut off the possibility of hearing God.

As we read the Scripture, it is especially important that we *hear* what's being said. This can be done only by focusing our attention on the words, letting them have impact on our conscious and subconscious minds. Silence allows this to happen. How unusual it was that afternoon on a busy street corner in Lincoln when I *heard* the psalmist say, "My heart is ready, O God!" God got through to me amidst the din of the city. I think that happened only once. But in the quiet of morning or evening devotions—alone with Scripture or a good book—those moments come with much more regularity. Then, too, in the imposed and sometimes awkward quiet of directed group prayer, such as those encouraged here, God can be heard breaking through both in the silence and in the prayers of others. May we heed the psalmist (Ps 130:6):

> My soul waits for the Lord
> > more than watchmen wait for the morning,
> > more than watchmen wait for the morning.

PRINCIPLES AND PRACTICE

In the final analysis, of course, these principles are not the thing. Practice is the thing. Have I seemed in this chapter to reduce prayer to principles? No. I haven't tried what can't be done. Prayer is practice. It is up to each of us and each of our communities to practice . . . practice . . . practice.

Appendix
Guide for Small Group Leaders

Small groups can learn to pray through the psalms. The procedure is similar to that of private prayer but takes place in community. Solitude is gone, but silence is still possible. Moreover, there is the added factor that when two or three are gathered together, Christ is there with you.

Learning to pray through the psalms does, of course, make demands on the group leader. The following suggestions should smooth the way to successful group experiences and spiritual growth for those who participate.

1. Come to the group prepared. Make this psalm your own answering speech. That is, work through the material in each chapter a few days before the group meets. This will give your experience with the psalm time to confirm itself in your own life.

2. Just before the group meets, review the relevant chapter and then answer the study questions preceding the group prayer liturgy. As you do so, imagine the sorts of answers and comments group members are likely to give. This anticipation will help you to handle any tough issues that may arise.

3. Be willing to participate in the discussion. You will not be lecturing;

instead you will be encouraging the members of the group to discuss what they have seen in the psalm.

4. Be sensitive to the other members of the group. Listen attentively when they describe what they are seeing. You may be surprised by their insights. Most questions do not have a single "right" answer. This is especially true of those relating to application or to personal experiences.

   When possible, link what you say to the comments of others. Also, be affirming whenever you can. This will encourage some of the more hesitant members of the group to participate.

5. Be careful not to dominate the discussion. We are sometimes so eager to express our thoughts that we leave too little opportunity for others. By all means participate, but encourage all others to do so as well.

6. When you lead the prayer, speak slowly and pause when a pause is called for. The silence that follows may be more important to the spiritual experience of the members than the time you are speaking. At first this silence may feel awkward to the members. Let them know that silence is important. With repeated experiences as you proceed through the psalms, the silence will feel less and less awkward. Participants may eventually tell you that the silences following the words of the psalm are the richest moments of the prayer.

7. Expect God to teach you through the psalm and through the preceding conversation among group members.

8. Comments made during the study will often reveal personal matters that are confidential and should not be discussed outside the group unless specific permission is given to do so. This should be made clear to the group at the beginning of each study.

9. At the end of the group prayer liturgy, some may want to say something about their personal experience. Give them freedom and time to
   do so. These comments may reveal personal problems. Let these comments spark practical responses that can be made in the next few days
   and weeks.

I have led many groups and been a participant in many more. I can say
with confidence that if you as a leader give heart and mind to personal
study and prayer, you will be greatly rewarded by what you see happening
in the lives of those who participate. May God give you great joy in serving him by helping others!

Notes

Introduction

p. 11   "And I was learning to pray": Oddly enough, that first edition of the new translation (the RSV) translates 108:1 as "My heart is ready, O God. My heart is ready," but later editions, like the 1962 edition I used for many years as my main study Bible, read "My heart is steadfast, O God. My heart is steadfast." It's a moot question whether I would have felt my heart was steadfast enough to immediately pray these lines. But I think not. The Hebrew word—so I am told by my IVP scholar-editor—can be translated either way. Who is to say which way produces an effect most similar to the intention of the ancient psalmist?

p. 11   "From their origin": Eugene Peterson, *Answering God* (San Francisco: HarperSanFrancisco, 1991), p. 54.

p. 13   "If we skip to analysis": I have written about this process in considerable depth in "Thinking by Reading," chap. 8 of *Habits of the Mind* (Downers Grove, Ill.: InterVarsity Press, 2000), pp. 147-77. See also my *How to Read Slowly* (Colorado Springs, Colo.: Shaw, 1978).

p. 13   "Louis Agassiz, a Harvard zoologist": Louis Menand, *The Metaphysical Club: The Story of Ideas in America* (New York: Farrar, Straus and Giroux, 2001), p. 100.

Chapter 1: Becoming Right with God

p. 29   "The assumption that prayer": Eugene Peterson, *Answering Prayer* (San Francisco: HarperSanFrancisco, 1992), p. 84.

Chapter 2: Waiting for the Lord

p. 36   "The French poet": Charles Baudelaire, "De Profoundis Clamavi" [Out of the depths I cry], in *Les Fleurs du Mal* [The Flowers of Evil], trans. Richard Howard (Boston: David R. Godine, 1982), pp. 36-37. This observation was suggested by Stanley L. Jaki, *Praying the Psalms* (Grand Rapids: Eerdmans, 2001), p. 217.

p. 38   "The very first line": Walter Brueggemann calls the opening line "a miserable cry of a nobody from nowhere" (*The Message of the Psalms* [Minneapolis: Augsburg, 1984], p. 104).

p. 42   "It is hoping": Brueggemann notes that "*wait* and *hope* are rough synonyms" (*Message*, p. 106).

p. 43   "Either we have hope": Václav Havel, *Disturbing the Peace: A Conversation with Karol Hvízdaka*, trans. Paul Wilson (New York: Alfred A. Knopf, 1990), p. 181.

Chapter 3: Night Thoughts

p. 57   "Psalm 4 has always": Stanley Jaki, *Praying the Psalms: A Commentary* (Grand Rapids: Eerdmans, 2001), p. 38.

p. 58   "Secrecy is the best opportunity": C. H. Spurgeon, *The Treasury of David* (Peabody, Mass.: Hendrickson, n.d.), 1:40.

Chapter 4: A Morning Meditation

p. 68   "This is the fittest time": C. H. Spurgeon, *The Treasury of David* (Peabody, Mass.: Hendrickson, n.d.), 1:46.

p. 74   "True, Old Testament scholar Peter Craigie": For example, Peter Craigie, *Psalms 1-50*, Word Biblical Commentary 19 (Waco, Tex.: Word, 1983), p. 87; and Spurgeon, *Treasury of David*, 1:47.

p. 74   "He calls for God": The apostle Paul cites these verses when he describes our sinful human condition in Romans 8:13.

Chapter 5: Thirsting for God

p. 85   "From even a cursory examination": Peter C. Craigie, *Psalms 1-50*, Word Biblical Commentary 19 (Waco, Tex.: Word, 1983), p. 325.

p. 85   "As the deer": I have chosen to use the New International Version because the translation of the first line yields for me the warmest emotional response. I also appreciate the King James Version: "As the hart panteth after the water brooks, so panteth my soul for thee, O God."

p. 90   "Old Testament scholar Peter Craigie": Craigie, *Psalms 1-50*, pp. 326-27. I have changed the verse numbers in this quotation from Craigie to match the numbering of the text I am using, the NIV.

p. 91   "Here is the picture": Derek Kidner, *Psalms 1-72* (Downers Grove, Ill.: InterVarsity Press, 1973), p. 167.

p. 91   "Billow followed billow": C. H. Spurgeon, *The Treasury of David* (Peabody, Mass.:

Hendrickson, n.d.), 1:274.

p. 91   "From the beginning": Leland Ryken, James C. Wilhoit and Tremper Longman
          III, eds., *The Dictionary of Biblical Imagery* (Downers Grove, Ill.: InterVarsity Press,
          1998), p. 201.

p. 95   "Kidner identifies the waterfall": Kidner, *Psalms 1-72*, p. 166.

p. 96   "these psalms are the 'lament'": Ibid., p. 165.

p. 97   "Still, Craigie states it": Craigie, *Psalms 1-50*, p. 325.

Chapter 6: A Plea for Deliverance from Slander

p. 113   "Scholars hesitate": Cush is unknown, but whoever he was, Charles Spurgeon
          says he probably "accused David to Saul of treasonable conspiracy against his
          royal authority" (C. H. Spurgeon, *The Treasury of David* [Peabody, Mass.: Hen-
          drickson, n.d.], 1:67). Peter Craigie notes that David had problems with other
          Benjaminites (Peter C. Craigie, *Psalms 1-50*, Word Biblical Commentary 19
          [Waco, Tex.: Word, 1983], p. 99).

p. 118   "The Psalms are all made up": Thomas Merton, *Praying the Psalms* (Collegeville,
          Minn.: Liturgical, 1956), p. 11.

Chapter 7: A Blazing Song of Joy

p. 128   "The Pearl of the Psalms": C. H. Spurgeon, *The Treasury of David* (Peabody,
          Mass.: Hendrickson, n.d.), 2:432-33.

p. 131   "The heading of the psalm": Marvin E. Tate, *Psalms 51-100*, Word Biblical
          Commentary 20 (Waco, Tex.: Word, 1990), p. 351.

p. 131   "Spurgeon suggests a tune": Spurgeon, *Treasury of David*, 2:432.

p. 131   "The Korahites": Tate, *Psalms 51-100*, p. 351.

p. 135   "Not *agape* love": I can't keep from quoting Spurgeon, the ever flowery exposi-
          tor: "He [the psalmist] had a holy lovesickness upon him and was wasted with
          an inward consumption because he was debarred the worship of the Lord in the
          appointed place. . . . It was God himself that he pined for, the only living and
          true God. His whole nature entered into his longing. Even the clay-cold flesh
          grew warm through the intense action of his fervent spirit" (Spurgeon, *Treasury
          of David*, 2:433).

Chapter 8: Praying Our Anger

p. 147   "As C. S. Lewis says": C. S. Lewis, *Reflections on the Psalms* (London: Fontana,
          1961), p. 23.

p. 149   "Every line of it": Derek Kidner, *Psalms 73-150: A Commentary on Books III-V of the Psalms*, Tyndale Old Testament Commentary (Grand Rapids: Eerdmans, 1975), p. 459.

p. 149   "No section of the Psalter": Dietrich Bonhoeffer, *Psalms: The Prayer Book of the Bible* (Minneapolis: Augsburg Fortress, 1974), p. 56.

p. 159   "a feature of ancient": Leslie C. Allen, *Psalms 101-150*, Word Biblical Commentary 21 (Waco, Tex.: Word, 1983), p. 237. Allen cites Nahum 3:10 and Isaiah 13:16; his reference to 2 Kings 8:2 should be 2 Kings 8:12. Lest we think humanity has progressed in moral sensitivity, we should note that in the twentieth century the Nazis used a similar method to exterminate Jewish children (see Kidner, *Psalms 73-150*, p. 460).

p. 160   "Jeremiah later prophesies": See R. K. Harrison, *Jeremiah and Lamentations: An Introduction and Commentary*, Tyndale Old Testament Commentary (Downers Grove, Ill.: InterVarsity Press, 1973), p. 223. "The sufferings of the people of Judah are described as though one man had experienced them" (ibid., p. 223). So likewise is the call for vengeance in Lamentations 3:55-63.

p. 160   "How can they sing these": Psalm 122 is another song of Zion.

p. 163   "The Lord Himself": Derek Kidner, *Psalms 1-72: A Commentary on Books I-II of the Psalms*, Tyndale Old Testament Commentary (Grand Rapids: Eerdmans, 1973), p. 31.

p. 164   "The reaction of the Psalmists": Lewis, *Reflections on the Psalms*, p. 27.

p. 165   "Our hate needs": Eugene Peterson, *Answering God: The Psalms as Tools for Prayer* (San Francisco: HarperSanFrancisco, 1989), p. 98.

p. 166   "Only in the cross": Bonhoeffer, *Psalms*, pp. 58-60.

Chapter 9: The God Who Knows Me

p. 177   "The crown of all the psalms": Quoted by John Stott, *The Canticles and Selected Psalms* (London: Hodder & Stoughton, 1966), p. 151.

p. 177   "This psalm contains": Stanley Jaki, *Praying the Psalms* (Grand Rapids: Eerdmans, 2001), p. 226.

p. 177   "The brightness of this Psalm": C. H. Spurgeon, *The Treasury of David* (Peabody, Mass.: Hendrickson, n.d.), 3:256; see Ezekiel 1:22.

p. 183   "He is in awe": Spurgeon says regarding the first line of this psalm: "It is ever the observer and the observed! Jehovah and me! Yet this most intimate connection exists, and therein lies our hope. Let the reader sit still a while and try to realize the two poles of this statement,—the Lord and poor puny man—and he will see much to admire and wonder at" (*Treasury of David*, 3:259).

p. 183   "Many Christian readers": Stott, *Canticles and Selected Psalms*, p. 153.

p. 184   "thrown in": C. S. Lewis, *Reflections on the Psalms* (London: Fontana, 1961), p. 24.

p. 184   "Some scholars think": See Leslie C. Allen, *Psalms 101-150*, Word Biblical Commentary 21 (Waco, Tex.: Word, 1983), pp. 260-63.

Chapter 10: Our Mighty Fortress

p. 208   "John Stott says": John Stott, *The Canticles and Selected Psalms* (London: Hodder & Stoughton, 1966), pp. 100, 102.

Chapter 11: Teach Us to Pray

p. 212   "No day in the life": Joachim Jeremias, *The Prayers of Jesus*, trans. John Bowden and Christoph Burchard (Philadelphia: Fortress, 1967), p. 74.

p. 213   "Some begin in agony": Psalm 22 is the most dramatic illustration of this. On the cross Jesus prayed the despairing first verse of this psalm. Jesus' resolution of his despair, reflected in "It is finished," echoes the final words of the psalm.

Annotated Bibliography

COMMENTARIES

The spiritual rewards of praying the psalms are partly dependent on the quality of one's understanding of the psalms themselves. Intensive, repetitive reading of the psalms comes first and is most important. Then comes digging into the backgrounds of each psalm, clarifying the meaning and identifying the places, people and events that occur in the text. Commentaries are the most convenient sources for help.

Derek Kidner's two volumes on the Psalms in the Tyndale Old Testament Commentary series have been for me the most helpful year after year: *Psalms 1-72* (1973) and *Psalms 73-150* (1975) are published by InterVarsity Press, Downers Grove, Illinois. These two volumes may be all you need for a rich experience of reading and praying the Psalms.

For a much deeper analysis, highly scholarly but still readable, I consult three volumes (19-21) of the Word Biblical Commentary: Peter C. Craigie, *Psalms 1-50* (1983); Marvin E. Tate, *Psalms 51-100* (1990); and Leslie C. Allen, *Psalms 101-150* (1983). They are published by Word Books, Dallas, Texas.

A briefer but also helpful commentary is found in the one-volume *New Bible Commentary*, edited by G. J. Wenham, J. A. Motyer, D. A. Carson and R. T. France, and published by InterVarsity Press. The section on the Psalms is written by Motyer.

For those like myself who just can't get enough of the Psalms, I highly recommend C. H. Spurgeon's *The Treasury of David*, first published in 1892 and reissued by Thomas Nelson, Nashville, Tennessee, in 1983. It not only contains Spurgeon's often flowery but nonetheless profound spiritual commentary on each verse of every psalm; it also collects "illustrative extracts" from a wide range of previous pastors and scholars who have written on the Psalms. It is a dipper's delight.

STUDIES OF THE PSALMS

One of the more prolific writers on the Psalms is Eugene Peterson, a longtime pastor and teacher. His *Answering Prayer* (1992) published by HarperSanFrancisco suggested a phrase (*answering speech*) and concepts used frequently in the present book; his comments on the imprecatory character of Psalm 137 have heavily influenced my own. Among his other expositions of the Psalms I recommend most highly *A Long Obedience in the Same Direction* (second edition, 2000), which reflects on the Psalms of Ascent (Psalms 120—134); it is published by InterVarsity Press. So is his *Earth & Altar* (1985), which examines eleven psalms for what they can contribute to "changing life in America." In addition, Peterson turns his paraphrasing and poetic powers on the Psalms in *The Message*. In 1994 a volume containing only the Psalms was published by NavPress, Colorado Springs, Colorado.

The overview and scholarly study of the Psalms I have found most helpful in writing the present book is *The Psalms: Their Structure and Meaning* by Pius Drijvers and published in 1964 by Herder and Herder, New York. It is out of print and probably unavailable but worth checking for in your local library or a used-book store.

Tremper Longman III's *How to Read the Psalms*, which covers much of the same ground as Drijvers's book, can take its place; it is published by

InterVarsity Press (1988).

Walter Brueggemann's *The Message of the Psalms* (1984), published by Augsburg in Minneapolis, Minnesota, is a rich theological commentary. Though Brueggemann classifies the Psalms in a rather eccentric way as psalms of orientation, disorientation and new orientation, I have found his insights helpful.

Dietrich Bonhoeffer's little book *Psalms: The Prayer Book of the Bible*, published by Augsburg in 1996, is a gem, highly recommended for its stimulating comments on learning to pray the psalms.

I have also found Thomas Merton's *Praying the Psalms* (1956) an encouraging and practical pamphlet well worth digesting slowly. It is published by The Liturgical Press, Collegeville, Minnesota.

Finally, I must mention C. S. Lewis's *Reflection on the Psalms* (1958), published by Harcourt, Brace in New York. It pains me to say this, but I think Lewis, in part because of his orientation as a classical scholar, in part because of what I think is his failure to grasp the ancient Hebrew character of the Psalms, has misunderstood some key aspects of the Psalms, especially the imprecatory psalms. I would not offer this caveat were his books much less known. Better for psalms readers to dip into Bonhoeffer or Merton.

BOOKS ON PRAYER AND OTHER SPIRITUAL DISCIPLINES

There are hundreds of books on prayer and the spiritual disciplines. I could recommend many. Instead I will just list two here. The first one by Dallas Willard taught me more about the meaning and character of the disciplines than any other. The second by David Hansen resonates more with the experience of my soul than any other.

I read Dallas Willard's *The Spirit of the Disciplines* when I was beginning a much needed five-month sabbatical from traveling, lecturing and teaching. I needed to stop and take a deep look at where I had come in my spiritual life. This is not a touchy-feely book but a theological inquiry into how God changes lives. It would make a great companion to those who are praying through the psalms. It was published by HarperSanFrancisco in 1988.

David Hansen is a poet in prose. His *A Little Handbook on Having a Soul* (1997) published by InterVarsity Press examines the spiritual character of the inner self, that from which our prayers emerge. While the book is unfortunately out of print, it may still be available at libraries or used-book stores—and it's worth the hunt. This book is black angus steak for the soul.

ormatio

**TRADITION. EXPERIENCE.
TRANSFORMATION.**

Formatio books from InterVarsity Press follow the rich tradition of the church in the journey of spiritual formation. These books are not merely about being informed, but about being transformed by Christ and conformed to his image. Formatio stands in InterVarsity Press's evangelical publishing tradition by integrating God's Word with spiritual practice and by prompting readers to move from inward change to outward witness. InterVarsity Press uses the chambered nautilus for Formatio, a symbol of spiritual formation because of its continual spiral journey outward as it moves from its center. We believe that each of us is made with a deep desire to be in God's presence. Formatio books help us to fulfill our deepest desires and to become our true selves in light of God's grace.